Table of Contents

Copyright Material

The Academy for Lease & Finance Professionals

Setting the Standards of Professionalism For Over 30 years

History & Overview
75 Points
25 Questions

1

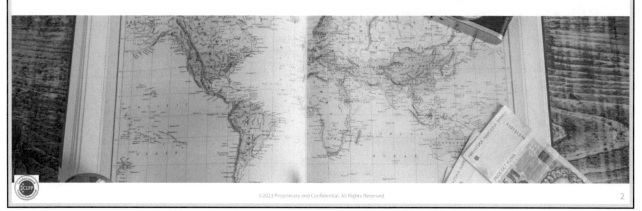

2010 B.C. to Present

History of Commercial Equipment Finance

2

2

Beginning of Leasing

- Oldest record – 2010 B.C. in the Sumerian City of Ur
  - Used clay tablets for documenting leases for agricultural tools, land and water rights, and oxen and other animals

- Around 1700 - 1750 B.C. - The Code of Hammurabi
  - King Hammurabi acknowledged leasing of personal property in his Code of Laws
  - First record of leasing law

3

Ship Charters

- Early example of a true lease
  - Phoenicians were shipping and trading experts who used ship charters to obtain a ship and crew
  - Other charters covered the economic life of the ship and required the lessee to assume the benefits and obligations of ownership

Statute of Wales

- English Common Law

- Used in England to deal directly with the leasing of personal property

- Further clarified in 1571 to define who actually owned the leased property

5

5

The Railroad Industry – Industrial Revolution

- In the UK and the United States, the railroad companies could only afford the track

- Sought financing from private investors for the locomotives and railcars
  - Accomplished through equipment trusts
  - Most well-known finance plan was the Philadelphia Plan

6

6

Early 1900s

- Independent 3rd Party leasing companies were formed to provide vendor financing for manufacturers

- Manufacturers saw the benefit of leasing to move product and gave rise to early captives

- At the start of WWII, the government used cost-plus contracts making leasing attractive again post-Depression

7

7

- Post WWII, there was an economic slump
  - The government tried to stimulate the economy and in 1953, Section 167 of the Internal Revenue Code was issued
  - Gave the owner/lessor the ability to take ordinary payments into income associated with a lease and accelerate depreciation
  - Designed to encourage capital spending

Shift to Modern Leasing (1950s)

8

IRS Revenue Ruling 55-540

① P (Payments > Rental): Rental payments are not substantially higher than a fair rental value

② A (Automatic Title): Ownership of the asset does not automatically pass to the lessee at the end of the term

③ I (Interest): No portion of the lease payment is characterized as interest

④ N (Nominal P.O.): The transaction does not include a nominal purchase option

⑤ E (Equity): No portion of the lease payments can be applied to an equity position in the asset

⑥ E (Excessive Payments): The amount paid under a short-term lease is not a significant portion of the purchase price (excessive lease payments)

9

1960s

- The Investment Tax Credit (ITC) was introduced
  - A credit that a taxpayer was permitted to claim on its federal tax return
  - Acted as a direct offset to tax liability as a result of ownership of qualified equipment

- In 1963, the Comptroller of the Currency gave banks the go-ahead to own and lease personal property
  - This brought a significant amount of capital held by banks into the leasing market

10

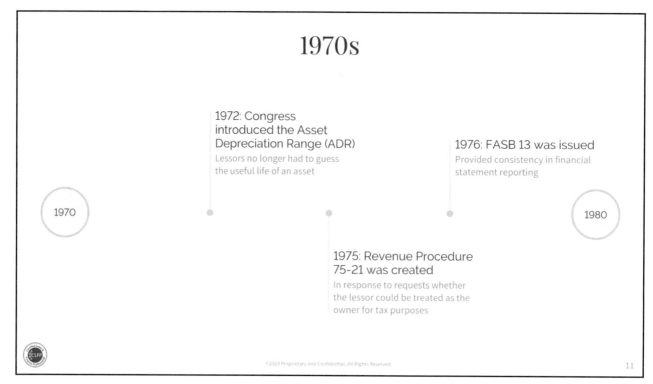

11

Revenue Procedure 2001-28

Supersedes Revenue Procedure 75-21
Used for advanced ruling purposes and all factors must be true for the lessor to be considered the owner
Failure to meet criteria may cause a transaction to be deemed a "mere financing"

- Initial minimum investment

- Lease term and renewal options

- Purchase and sale rights

- No investment by lessee

- No lease loans or guarantees

- Profit requirement

12

12

ASC 842

 Title to the property automatically transfers to the lessee by or at the end of the lease term

 The lease contains a bargain purchase option

 The lease term is equal to or greater than 75% of the estimated economic life of the leased property

 The present value of the minimum lease payments at the beginning of the lease term is equal to or greater than 90% of the fair market value of the property

 The underlying asset is of a specialized nature

13

13

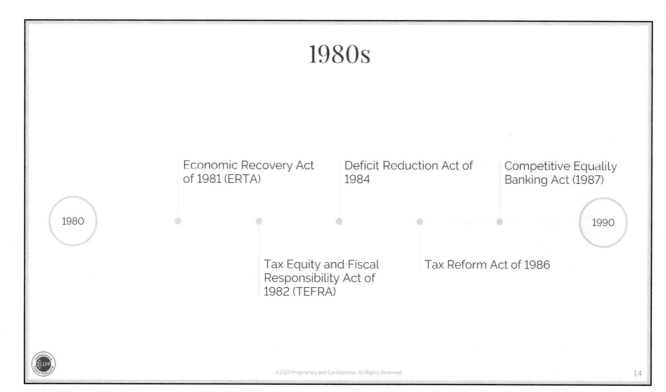

1980s

14

14

Economic Recovery Tax Act (ERTA) – 1981

- Revision to the Internal Revenue Code; it replaced the more complex Asset Depreciation Range (ADR) system

- Created the Accelerated Cost Recovery System (ACRS)
  - Only five classes of assets, ranging from 3 – 15 year life spans
  - The owner/lessor could now fully depreciate an asset without having to estimate useful life and salvage value

15

15

Tax Reform Act of 1986 (TRA '86)

- Strengthened and expanded the reach of the Alternative Minimum Tax (AMT)
  - A company must do a third calculation using the AMT formula and pay the greater of the regular tax calculation or of AMT
  - Under AMT, there are limits to depreciation

- Eliminated the Investment Tax Credit (ITC)

16

16

1990s

- Credit Scoring Innovation
  Independents led the charge, followed by some captives and finally banks

- Third Party Originators (TPO)
  TPOs were now accepted by banks

- Creative Financing Structures & Large-Ticket Leasing
  - FMV, PUT, 1st Amendment Leases and other creative leasing structures grew
  - Independent and captive leasing companies sought to distinguish themselves from the banks

17

Creative Large-Ticket Transaction Structures

Double-Dip Lease
- Based on cross-border leases, but structured to take advantage of tax benefits in both the lessee and lessor's country

Leveraged Lease
- Unique mix of tax and accounting benefits
- Up to 97% of recourse and nonrecourse debt is used to finance the assets
- Created high returns on equity to the lessor which allowed the lessor to offer lower rates

Synthetic Lease
- Designed to be a loan for tax purposes, but an operating lease for accounting purposes
- Still in existence today

18

2000s

- Technology investment rapidly drove the market up; however in 2001 with the dot-com burst the software sector transactions failed

- The Enron collapse led to increased regulatory scrutiny and changes in accounting rules for leases, financial reporting requirements, and accounting for public companies
  - Highlighted the need to enact Sarbanes-Oxley

19

The NorVergence Program

- Massive case of telecom equipment fraud with widespread industry impact

- There was a crowd mentality of credit, "If company X approves it, we should be able to as well"

- The Hell or High-Water clause did not hold up in many jurisdictions because courts thought the equipment specialists should have known better

- The equipment was worth 10% or less than the amount financed

- Changed the concept of financing for services included in leases

20

2010 – Present

- 2010 - Consumer Financial Protection Bureau (CFPB) was created by the Dodd-Frank Wall Street Reform and Consumer Protection Act
  - Although designed to protect consumers, many laws are written to apply to smaller equipment financing transactions

- The number one equipment financing company in the world, GE, exited the industry

- Cloud-based technology and FinTech gained momentum

21

21

Overview of the Commercial Equipment Industry

22

Equipment Lease Definition

A transaction in which use and possession, but not title to tangible property, is transferred for consideration

23

23

Market Segment	Small-Ticket	Middle/Mid-Ticket	Large-Ticket	
Typical Transaction Size	<$250,000	<$5,000,000	>$5,000,000	Industry Sector by Transaction Size
Notes	Under $25,000 often called "micro-ticket"	Between $250,000 and $1MM often called "Lower Middle-Market"	Often referred to as "Big-Ticket"	
Examples	Micro: credit card machines, laptops, computers, etc. Small: trucks, trailers, medical equipment, etc.	Fleet vehicles, CNC machine tools, agricultural equipment, etc.	Rail cars, aircraft, marine, etc.	

24

Industry Participants

 Equipment End-Users
Borrower/Lessee

 Regulators
IRS, CFPB, etc.

 Third Party Originators
Brokers, Alternative lenders, etc.

 Trade Associations
AACFB, CLFP, ELFA, NEFA, etc.

 Lessors & Lenders
Suppliers of the finance produce

 Service Companies
Software, insurance, UCC filings, etc.

 Investors
Capital market buyers and sellers

 Equipment Suppliers
Dealers, vendors, etc.

25

Government Leasing

- Three categories
  - Municipal leasing
  - Leases to the federal government
  - Lease to Native American tribes and nations

- Each is subject to unique tax implications, documentation, structure, and early termination requirements

- The interest paid by a municipal government for public purposes is normally not subject to federal income tax

26

Competition to Equipment Financing

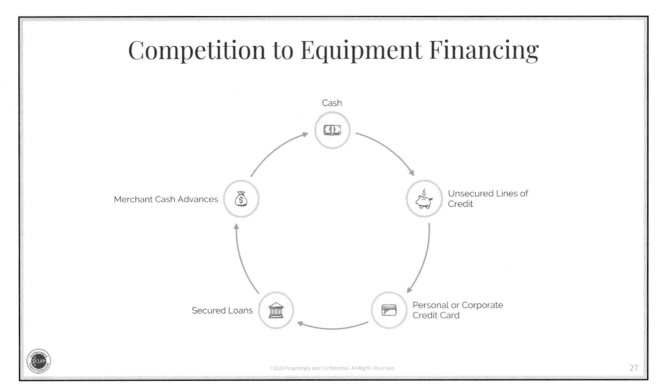

27

Alternative Funding

Merchant Cash Advance

- Typically for transactional/retail-oriented small businesses
- Borrower receives an advance on future credit card receivables

Working Capital

- Short-term, unsecured loans often used as a complement to a lease
- Gives quick access to funds to run or grow a business
- Allows for flexibility in the ways the borrower may use the funds

Invoice Factoring

- Does not involve financing, but accelerates the cash flow of the business in exchange for a slight discount on the face value of the invoice
- It's an off-balance sheet method of financing

28

The Three Lenses for Examining Leases

Tax

IRS determines the eligibility for tax benefits (IRS Rev. Ruling 55-540)

"Tax Lease" or "Conditional Sales Obligation"

Accounting

FASB determines eligibility (ASC 842)

Lessee: "Operating Lease" or "Finance Lease"

Lessor: "Operating Lease," "Sales-type Lease," or "Direct Financing Lease"

Legal

UCC and court systems determine eligibility

"True Lease," "Finance Lease," or "Conditional Sales Contract"

29

29

Names for Equipment Finance Products

30

Commercial Term Loan
- A loan agreement between a business and financial insitution with a fixed maturity date and stipulated periodic payments

Conditional Sales Contract
- Agreement for the purchase of an asset and the lessee is treated as the owner for federal income tax purposes

Equipment Finance Agreement
- Resembles the structure of a finance lease, but provides for the lender to lend the borrower an amount for the purchase of the equipment (typically, lender pays the vendor invoice and files a lien against the collateral)

Finance Lease
- This term is used in many forms and one is often confusingly used to refer to a conditional sale in the form of a lease transaction

31

31

Leveraged Lease
- Involves at a minimum, a lessee, lessor, and funding source from which the lessor borrows a significant portion of the cost of the equipment

Fair Market Value Lease (FMV)
- A lease which contains an option for the lessee to purchase the leased property at the end of the term for fair market value (the price that a willing seller and buyer negotiate in an open marketplace)

Net Lease
- All costs in connection with the use of the property are paid separately by the lessee and are not included in the rental payment to the lessor

Money-Over-Money Lease
- A non-tax lease or conditional sales contract in the guise of a lease, in which the title is intended to pass to the lessee at the end of the lease term

Operating Lease
- Accounting term that fails to meet any of the ASC 842 criteria

32

32

Non-Tax Lease

- Any lease in which the lessee is, or will become, the owner during or at the end of the lease term and is entitled to all the tax benefits of ownership

Purchase Upon Termination (PUT)

- Lessee agrees to buy and the lessor agrees to sell the equipment for a predetermined amount upon termination of the lease

Rental Agreement

- A short service lease; typically less than 12 months

Sale-Leaseback

- Transaction in which the original user sells an asset to a lessor and then leases it back

TRAC Lease

- A lease on a qualified automobile, truck or trailer which is considered a true lease for federal income tax even though it has a Terminal Rental Adjustment Clause (TRAC) which effectively guarantees the residual value

33

Benefits of Leasing

Cash Flow Management

- Up to 100% of equipment cost may be financed
- Improved cash forecasting

Tax Benefits

- May be a faster deduction from rent expenses
- 100% expensing on money over money leases

Financial Reporting

Ratio enhancement, higher earnings, and increased cash flow and working capital*

*Operating leases only

Hedge Against Obsolescence

Ability to upgrade outdated equipment, refresh technology and terminate early *

*Operating leases only

Convenience & Flexibility

- Availability of financing, quick approval times
- Financial diversification
- Avoiding single obligor limits

34

The Academy for Lease & Finance Professionals

Setting the Standards of Professionalism For Over 30 years

Leasing Law
75 Points
25 Questions

1

Overview of Leasing Law

Statutory Law
- Federal Law - adopted by US Congress (e.g., Internal Revenue Code, Bankruptcy Code)
- State Law – adopted by State legislators (e.g., Sales Tax, UCC)

Case Law
- Cases that apply statutory law or prior case law precedents to particular sets of facts
- Type of law created by applying these precedents is called "common law"

Regulatory Law
- Regulations adopted by state and federal government regulatory agencies (e.g., IRS or SEC)
- Not binding upon the courts in the manner of statutory laws and may be subject to a judge's interpretation

2

2

Contract Law

- Generally a matter of state law

- Requirements include:
  - Offer and acceptance with mutual agreement on terms
  - Consideration (i.e., something of value given or promised)
  - Capacity (i.e., each of the parties are legally able to enter the contract)
  - Legality (e.g., usury, illegal activities)

3

Statute of Frauds

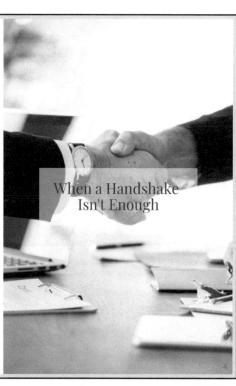

When a Handshake Isn't Enough

- Certain types of contracts are not enforceable, unless in writing

- Under the UCC, lease contracts with total payments in excess of $1,000 are unenforceable, unless in writing

4

Conflicts of Law and Choice of Law

Conflicts of Law
- Refers to inconsistencies in laws from state to state (e.g., the UCC is not uniform across all fifty states)
- Under this concept, a court chooses to apply the law of one state over that of another

Choice of Law
- Refers to a voluntary choice of the law of one jurisdiction to apply to a contract for another jurisdiction
- Avoids the need for a judge to make a conflicts of law decision

5

Legal Definition of a Lease

Differs from those for federal income tax and accounting purposes

Found in the Uniform Commercial Code (UCC)

Not a definition of what **IS** a lease, rather what it is **NOT**

A commercial equipment lease for legal purposes must be non-cancelable

6

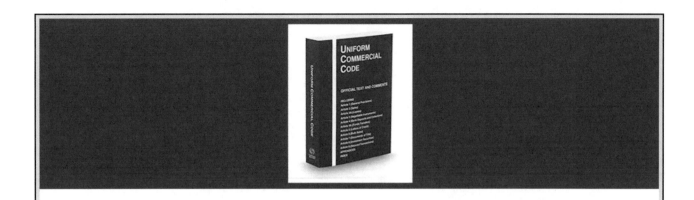

Uniform Commercial Code

Article 2, 9, 2a (10 in California)

7

Article 2

- Oldest article of the UCC in terms of equipment leasing and financing - introduced in the early 1960s

- Deals exclusively with sales of goods (tangible personal property)

- Comes into play when the lessor may be deemed a vendor or supplier under a secured loan financing

8

8

Article 2

- Source of "implied warranties"
  - Merchant who sells goods (lessor) is deemed to warrant that they are fit for ordinary purposes, in overall good condition, and fit for the particular use
  - May be excluded by a conspicuous disclaimer

9

9

Article 9

- Regulations for secured transactions; not true leases

- Sets up a system for recording personal property known as a UCC-1 Financing Statement

- Governs rights in goods (including equipment) used as collateral for loans

10

10

Article 9

- True leases do NOT need to have a UCC-1 filed, but it is a good idea in case the deal is held to be a loan

- Does not cover all types of claims and equipment (aircraft, vessels, vehicles, and certain other types of property are not covered)

- File in the state where the lessee is incorporated

- Key issue: first to file generally has priority

- Name of the "debtor" must be perfectly correct

11

UCC 1-203

Provides that a transaction always creates a security interest and is not a lease if **the lessee cannot terminate the lease** and any one of the following:

- The lease term equals or exceeds the equipment's economic life

- The lessee is required to buy the equipment, has a nominal purchase option, or automatically owns the equipment at the end of the lease term

- The lessee is required to renew the lease or has a nominal renewal amount and the renewal causes the lease term to equal or exceed the economic life of the equipment

12

Purchase Money Security Interest

- Exception to the UCC rule of first-to-file wins

- PMSI is a security interest or claim on property that enables a lender who provides financing to obtain priority ranking ahead of other secured creditors

- PMSI has priority over earlier filed ("perfected") security interest

- Must file in the state where the lessee is incorporated

- Must file within 20 days of DELIVERY of equipment to lessee

- Lessor must enable lessee to acquire the equipment (lessor must pay vendor; any down payment reimbursed to lessee is not protected by PMSI rule)

13

13

PMSI Example

- A Bank has a blanket lien on all assets of a lessee. The lessee signs a $1 purchase option lease with a lessor who pays 100% of the cost to the vendor and then files 19 days after the equipment was delivered to the lessee. In the event of a default, who will get the equipment?

14

14

Article 2a (10 in California)

- Deals only with "true leases"

- Includes "implied warranties"

- Similar to Article 2, the lessee may waive implied warranties through a conspicuous disclaimer

- A UCC-1 does not need to be filed since it is a "true lease," but it is a good idea

15

Article 2a (10 in California)

Introduces the term "finance Lease" - a true lease in which:

(1) The lessor is not the manufacturer or vendor ("supplier") of the leased property

(2) The lessor makes sure that the lessee is apprised of its rights against the supplier with respect to warranties

(3) The lessor does not select the equipment or lease it from an inventory of like items

16

Article 2a Warranties

Express Warranties

- Any affirmation of fact or promise made by the lessor to the lessee

Implied Warranties

- Quiet possession (use of the equipment as long as the lessee makes payments)
- Free from rightful claims of another
- Merchantability = goods must pass for goods of that type
- Fitness for a particular purpose

17

Contrasting the True Lease & Lease Intended as Security

	True Lease	Lease intended as Security
Distinctions in Bankruptcy	- Lessor has better rights to recover the equipment - Lessee cannot pursue a "cramdown" plan	Borrower may face a "cramdown", which may limit the lender's recover to the FMV of the equipment only
Interest/Usury	- Rent includes an interest factor - Usury laws do not apply in most states	Because interest is charged, payments may be subject to state usury limitations
Collateral	Inappropriate to refer to leased equipment as collateral	Appropriate to refer to financed equipment as collateral
Liability of Lessee and Lessor	More exposure to the lessor for liability to third parties caused by faulty or improperly maintained equipment	Less exposure to the lender for liability to third parties caused by faulty or improperly maintained equipment
UCC Rights	Governed by UCC Article 2A, Lessor owns	Governed by UCC Article 9, lender has security interest
Perfecting Security Interest in Different Types of Collateral	- Lessor not required to file a UCC-1 - Titled leases require the lessor to be shown as the owner on titles	- Lender should file a UCC-1 - Titled leases require notations to indicate interest
Residual	Lessors expect profit from rents and residual	Lenders look only to interest during the term

18

The Academy for Lease & Finance Professionals

Setting the Standards of Professionalism For Over 30 years

Sales & Marketing
75 Points
22 Questions

1

Marketing vs. Sales

Marketing

- Big picture marketing strategy and brand identity
- Generate awareness of the company, products, and solutions
- Use a variety of methods to generate leads
- Support the sales effort and play a significant role in stimulating the sales process
- Occurs before a sale is made and after the sale to pave the way for future referrals and sales
- Marketing activities should be used throughout the lifecycle to retain and incite return customers

Sales

- The act of influencing a customer to buy a product or service
- Convert the leads generated through marketing into sales
- Sales role requires utilizing the company's strengths and goals to determine the target market
- Identifying prospective customers by the type of account, by company size or structure (public, private, small or medium business, etc.), industry, equipment type, average transaction size, credit quality, and location

2

2

Marketing

The process of finding, developing, and profiting from opportunities

3

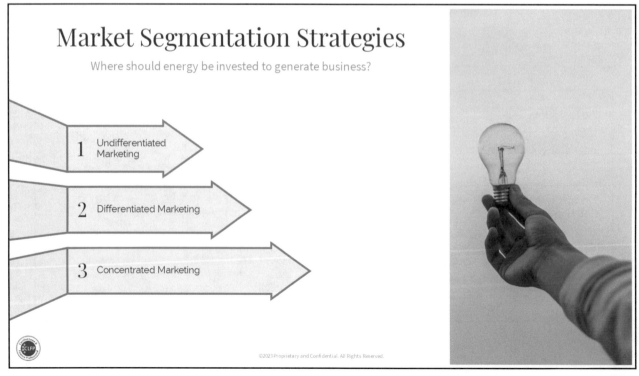

Market Segmentation Strategies

Where should energy be invested to generate business?

1 Undifferentiated Marketing

2 Differentiated Marketing

3 Concentrated Marketing

4

Market Segmentation Strategies

Undifferentiated Marketing
Go after the whole market with a product and marketing strategy intended to have mass appeal

Differentiated Marketing
Operate in several segments of the market with offerings and market strategy tailored to each segment

Concentrated Marketing
Focus on only one or a few segments with the intention of capturing a large share of these segments

5

5

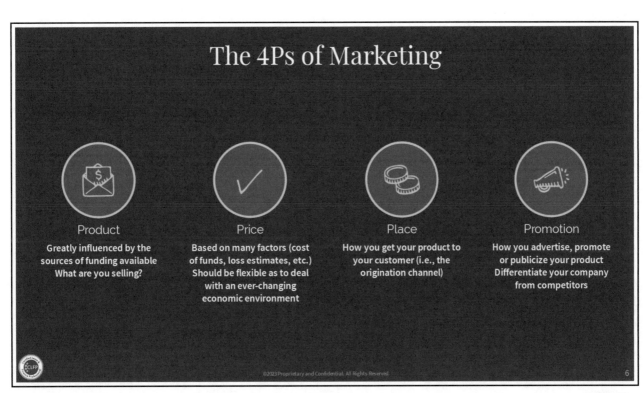

6

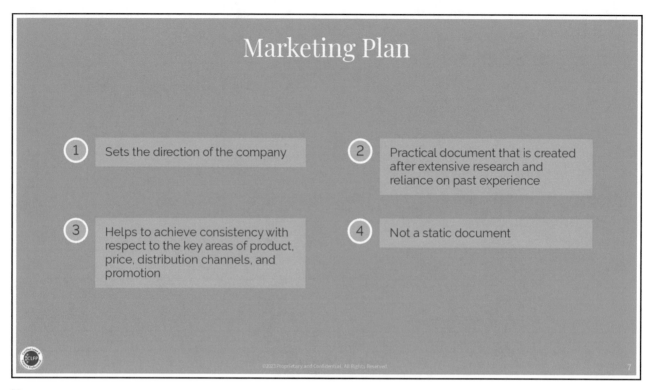

7

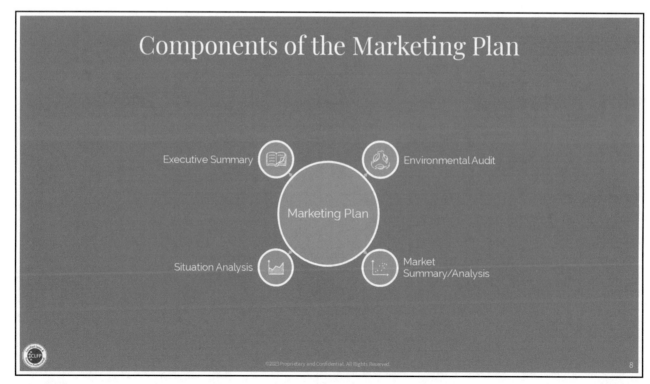

Executive Summary

Highlights the research and a statement of the future direction of the company

Allows the reader to understand the basics of product, price, promotion, place, and the general overall direction of the company

Great place for the Mission Statement

Statement of the overall goals of the company

Sets the direction of the organization

9

9

Situation Analysis

1 Market Summary

2 Environmental Audit

3 Funding

4 Keys to Success

5 Critical Issues

6 Credit Quality

7 Historical Results

10

10

11

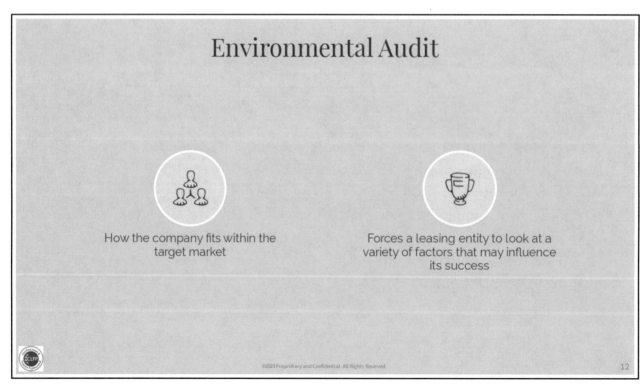

12

Keys to Successful Execution

Critical Issues
Challenges to address for the plan to work (e.g., hiring needs)

Historical Results
Detail past plans, successes, failures and performance measurements

Financials
Covers the specifics of projected volume, revenue, expenditures, profit, and rates of return as well as balance sheet concerns

Marketing Strategy
Once there is an understanding of the marketplace and where the lessor fits in, a strategy needs to be developed for how to be successful

13

The Sales Process

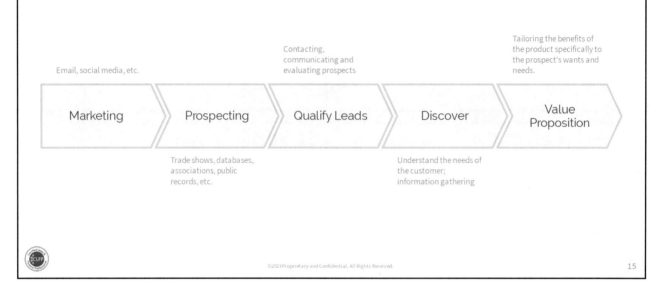

Email, social media, etc.

Contacting, communicating and evaluating prospects

Tailoring the benefits of the product specifically to the prospect's wants and needs.

Marketing → Prospecting → Qualify Leads → Discover → Value Proposition

Trade shows, databases, associations, public records, etc.

Understand the needs of the customer; information gathering

15

15

The Proposal

Typically includes:

- Parties to the transaction
- Type of transaction
- Payment terms
- Purchase/renewal terms
- Credit requirements
- Residual treatment
- Tax/insurance requirements
- Equipment description

- Equipment cost and expected delivery/funding dates
- Fees/miscellaneous transaction costs
- Expiration date of the proposal
- Documentation requirements
- Any additional requirements
- Disclaimer that it is only a proposal, not a commitment
- Place for the prospect to formally accept the proposal

16

16

Integration of Sales & Marketing Efforts

Brand

Top of Mind Awareness

Continuous Contact

17

17

Equipment Finance Origination Channels
Direct, Vendor and Third-Party Origination

18

Direct Origination

Lessor's own internal sales professionals

Lessor focuses on training internal sales professionals on credit parameters and products

The primary customer is the end-user of the equipment

Objective is meeting the needs of the customer by differentiating on customization, customer experience, and relationship throughout the lifecycle of the transaction

May use a Master Agreement to meet the specific repeat buying needs of the customer

19

Direct Origination Challenges for Companies with Multiple Finance Lines of Business

Exposure and Concentration Limits

Relationship Management

Relationship managers for other lending lines may set mixed expectations with the customer on rate or other elements of the transaction due to differences between their product and equipment financing

The Domain of Expertise

A challenge for captive leasing sales reps is the limitation on what types of equipment they can finance

20

Direct Origination Benefits and Drawbacks

Benefits

Efficiency in targeting the right type of business
Control over resources
Direct contact with lessee
Lessor can provide more services
For banks, it enables more relationship opportunities with its customers

Drawbacks

May be less efficient (cold calling)
Exposure limitations for larger financial institutions
"Golden Goose" customer
Limitation of a single funding source may lead to a lack of solution variety

21

Vendor Origination

 The vendor's sales-force or dealer representatives are the salespeople

 Lessor may provide private labeled documents, online tools, residual sharing, etc.

 Lessor focuses on educating the vendor organization on the program

 Typically some sort of written document between the lessor and vendor is agreed upon and outlines how the organizations will work together

 Lessor aims to generate a reliable quality flow of business that fits the goals of the organization

22

Typical Vendor Program Features

- Online portals for vendors to interact with the lessor

- Online portals for lessees to manage their contract obligation

- Training for vendor salespeople

- Private label where lessor provides financing in the name of the vendor

- Subsidized rate arrangements (e.g., 0% financing)

- Specialized invoicing features

- Lease contract documentation specific to the vendor program agreement

- Right of First Refusal (lessor has option to accept/reject all new applications from vendor)

24

Mitigating Risk with Vendor Programs

Remarketing agreements
The vendor agrees to sell or lease the equipment to another party upon termination of the lease or default by the lessee

Hold back agreements
A portion of the invoice proceeds due the vendor, is "held back" to mitigate risk
Once the contract is "seasoned," the vendor receives the "hold back" portion

Buy back agreements
Vendor agrees to repurchase the property from the lessor if a certain event occurs within a specified period of time

Ultimate Net Loss (UNL)
Pools of shared risk

25

Benefits of Vendor Origination

- The lessor can scale the sales effort with a higher return on time investment

- The lessor acquires a customer with whom they may potentially generate multiple deals

- It creates "stickiness" to drive return customer business to both the vendor and lessor

- Financing programs help vendors to move more of their product so that they can control the sale

- By focusing on a monthly payment, vendor sales people can often upsell the customer creating the opportunity for a larger sale

- It may generate a steady stream of business in an industry that fits your portfolio goals

- When compared to other origination channels, vendor programs generally perform better

- For the vendor, the ability to offer financing options can be a competitive advantage when compared to other vendors

26

Drawbacks of Vendor Origination

- Fraud (collusion of vendor and lessee; collusion of vendor and leasing sales representatives; lessee fraud)

- Temptation for lessor to lessen credit and documentation standards to provide a simpler, easier approval process

- Vendor relationship may put pressure on the lessor to approve transactions they typically would not

- Resource intensive for the lessor

- Lessor may become too dependent on a vendor

27

27

The Third-Party Origination Channel (TPO)

TPO: brokers, independent lessors, and other types of organizations that refer opportunities to finance companies for funding

Purpose is to widen transaction origination opportunities and increase portfolio diversity without having a direct sales team

From a broker's perspective, their primary role is to coordinate the end-to-end details of a transaction on behalf of the customer

Cost is higher because of the cost to buy the third-party business

28

28

Day in the Life of a Broker

Assuming the deal is approved

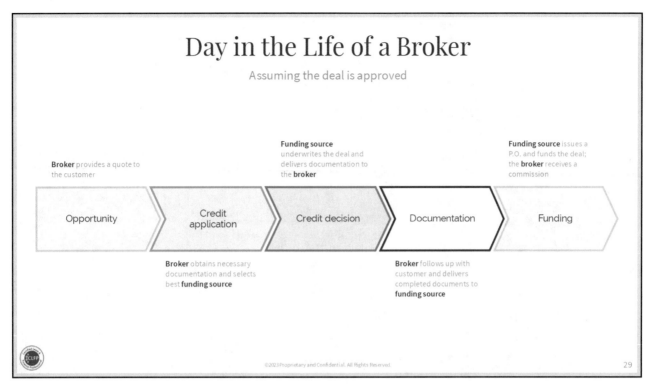

Broker provides a quote to the customer

Funding source underwrites the deal and delivers documentation to the **broker**

Funding source issues a P.O. and funds the deal; the **broker** receives a commission

Opportunity	Credit application	Credit decision	Documentation	Funding

Broker obtains necessary documentation and selects best **funding source**

Broker follows up with customer and delivers completed documents to **funding source**

29

Benefits of TPO Origination

Funding Source

- Outsources the sales effort
- Consistent stream of business that meets credit and portfolio criteria
- Documentation may be more reliable
- TPO is incented to manage the relationship and solve problems resulting in fewer headaches for the lessor

TPO

- Fund transactions without having to incur debt or use cash
- Less overhead and administration
- Develop a network of sources to solve client needs

30

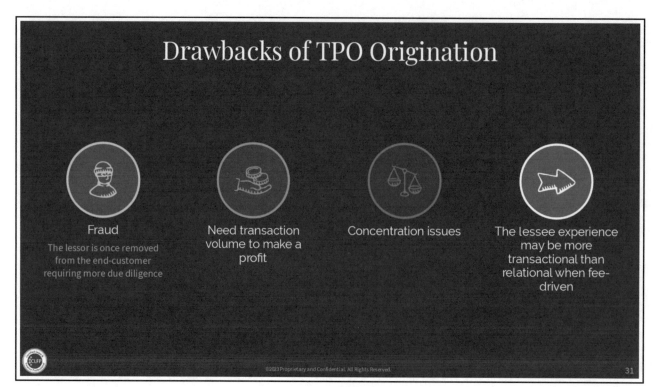

31

The Academy for Lease & Finance Professionals

Setting the Standards of Professionalism For Over 30 years

Financial & Tax Accounting
100 Points
37 Questions

1

Financial Statements vs. Tax Returns

- Do not always present the same results because:
  A given lease may be classified differently for book than for tax

  Financial statements are prepared using the accrual method of accounting

  Tax returns may be prepared using the cash method of accounting

  Rules governing how certain items, including depreciation, may be accounted for are distinctly different between "book" and "tax" accounting

2

2

Sales-Type Lease Accounting (ASC 842)

If any of the following criteria are present, the lease is considered a sales-type lease by the lessor

1. Automatic Title

2. Bargain purchase option

3. Lease term equal to or greater than 75% of the estimated economic useful life of the property

4. PV of the lease payments is equal to or greater than 90% of the FMV

5. The leased equipment is of such a specialized nature that only the lessee can use it without major modifications

3

3

Section 1

Classification under ASC 842

4

Operating or Sales-Type Lease?

Lessor's Perspective

1. Lease of MRI machine with a term of 36 months. Residual estimated to be 60% of original price. Lessee has option to purchase at lease termination for 4% and lessor's yield is 14%.

2. Lease of telescope with a term of 24 months. FMV option and lessor's yield is 9%. Economic life is estimated at 36 months.

3. Lease of laptop with a term of 48 months. An agreement between lessor and lessee to transfer title at termination of lease at no cost. Lessor's yield is 8.5%

5

5

Lease Classification for Tax Purposes (IRS)

Revenue Ruling 55-540 – the presence of any of the following could make a given transaction not a tax (true) lease:

1. The total amount of payments is an inordinately large portion of the sum required to be paid to secure title (in relation to the corresponding residual)

2. Automatic title

3. Some portion of the payment is designated as interest

4. Nominal purchase option

5. Portion of payment applied to equity position and not included in the lease

6. The "rental" payments greatly exceed the current fair rental value

6

6

Revenue Procedure 2001-28

Because Revenue Ruling 55-540 defined a contract of sale and did not include attributes of a lease, Revenue Procedure was issued by the IRS.

Risk
The lessor must maintain a minimum unconditional at-risk equity investment in the property during the lease term

Loans
The lessee may not lend any money to the lessor or guaranty the loan to buy the property

Right to Buy
The lessee may not have a contractual right to buy the property at less than the fair market value when the right is exercised

Investment
The lessee may **not** invest in the property

Profit
The lessor expects to receive profit

7

7

IRS Codes

Section 38 Property
Personal property that can be leased as depreciable property

Section 179
Allows a taxpayer to potentially deduct the full cost of an asset in the year the asset is placed in service

At-Risk
Requires the party seeking benefits such as interest deduction and depreciation to actually be "at-risk" for certain specified amounts

8

8

Financial Statements

Income Statement

Revenue	102,887	118,886	131,345	142,341	150,772	158,311	165,435	172,052
Cost of Goods Sold (COGS)	39,023	48,004	49,123	52,654	56,710	58,575	61,211	61,939
Gross Profit	62,984	70,882	82,222	89,687	94,062	99,736	104,224	110,113
Expenses								
Salaries and Benefits	26,427	22,658	23,872	23,002	25,245	26,913	28,124	29,249
Rent and Overhead	10,963	10,125	10,087	11,020	11,412	10,000	10,000	10,000
Depreciation & Amortization	19,500	18,150	17,205	16,544	16,080	15,008	15,005	15,003
Interest	2,500	2,500	1,500	1,500	1,500	1,500	1,500	500
Total Expenses	59,390	53,433	52,664	52,066	54,237	53,421	54,629	54,752
Earnings Before Tax	3,594	16,649	29,558	37,622	39,825	46,314	49,595	55,361
Taxes	1,120	4,858	8,483	10,908	11,598	12,968	13,887	15,501
Net Earnings	2,474	11,791	21,075	26,713	28,227	33,346	35,708	39,860

Balance Sheet

Assets								
Cash	167,971	181,210	183,715	211,069	239,550	272,530	307,632	327,097
Accounts Receivable	5,100	5,904	6,587	7,117	7,539	7,807	8,158	8,485
Inventory	7,805	9,801	9,825	10,531	11,342	11,715	12,242	12,388
Property & Equipment	45,500	42,350	40,145	38,602	37,521	37,513	37,508	37,505
Total Assets	226,376	239,065	240,252	267,319	295,951	329,564	365,540	385,474
Liabilities								
Accounts Payable	3,902	4,800	4,912	5,265	5,671	5,938	6,205	6,279
Debt	50,000	50,000	30,000	30,000	30,000	30,000	30,000	10,000
Total Liabilities	53,902	54,800	34,912	35,265	35,671	35,938	36,205	16,279
Shareholder's Equity								
Equity Capital	170,000	170,000	170,000	170,000	170,000	170,000	170,000	170,000
Retained Earnings	2,474	14,265	35,340	62,053	90,280	123,627	159,335	199,195
Shareholder's Equity	172,474	184,265	205,340	232,053	260,280	293,627	329,335	369,195
Total Liabilities & Shareholder's Equity	226,376	239,065	240,252	267,319	295,951	329,564	365,540	385,474
Check	0.000	0.000	0.000	0.000	0.000	0.000	0.000	0.000

Cash Flow Statement

Operating Cash Flow								
Net Earnings	2,474	11,791	21,075	26,713	28,227	33,346	35,708	39,860
Plus: Depreciation & Amortization	19,500	18,150	17,205	16,544	16,080	15,008	15,005	15,003
Less: Changes in Working Capital	9,003	1,702	775	903	827	375	611	398
Cash from Operations	12,971	28,239	37,505	42,354	43,480	47,980	50,102	54,465
Investing Cash Flow								
Investments in Property & Equipment	15,000	15,000	15,000	15,000	15,000	15,000	15,000	15,000
Cash from Investing	15,000	15,000	15,000	15,000	15,000	15,000	15,000	15,000

9

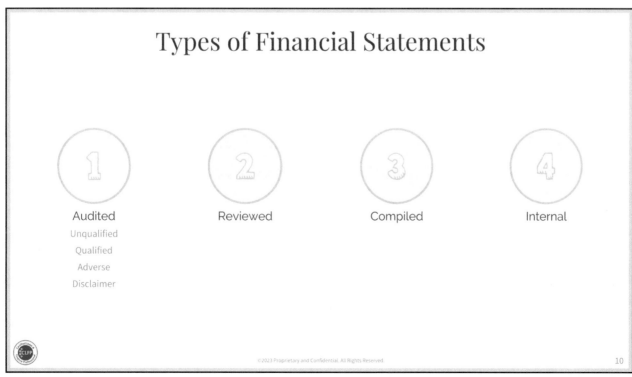

Types of Financial Statements

1 Audited
Unqualified
Qualified
Adverse
Disclaimer

2 Reviewed

3 Compiled

4 Internal

10

Compiled Statement

- Lowest level of assurance services

- Conducted in accordance with Statements on Standards for Accounting and Review Services issued by the AICPA (American Institute of CPAs)

- Limited to presenting in the form of financial statements information that is the representation of management

11

11

Reviewed Statement

- Next level of assurance services

- Conducted in accordance with Statements on Standards for Accounting and Review Services issued by the AICPA

- Consists principally of inquiries of company personnel and analytical procedures applied to financial data

- Procedures-driven engagement with limited assurance provided regarding the financial statements

12

12

Audited Statement

- Satisfies external reporting requirements for lending institutions and regulatory agencies

- Highest level of financial statement assurance service with an opinion of the fairness of the presentation

- May only be prepared and issued by an independent and properly licensed CPA firm or CPA

13

Audited Statement

Unqualified Opinion vs. Qualified Opinion

Unqualified Opinion	Qualified Opinion
Full audit has been performed	Full audit has been performed
Statements are according to GAAP	Statements are according to GAAP
Fairly represent the company's financial status	Fairly represent the company's financial status
	There are certain noted items that may be of concern

14

Audited Statement

Adverse Opinion and Disclaimer of Opinion

Adverse Opinion

Full audit has been performed

Statements do not comply with GAAP

Statements do NOT fairly represent the company's financial status

Disclaimer of Opinion

Not technically an 'opinion;' simply states that auditors chose not to issue an opinion

May be used when:

Auditor believes they cannot audit impartially (they recuse themselves)

Auditor's scope is limited (can't access certain data)

Auditors have other doubts

15

Key Components of the Financial Statement

Accountant's Letter

Balance Sheet

Income Statement and Net Income

Statement of Cash Flows

Accountant's Notes

16

Accountant's Letter

- Opening page and addressed to Board of Directors for corporation, general partner for partnership or the owner of a sole proprietorship

- Confirms that the statements are prepared in accordance with GAAP

17

Balance Sheet

Example Company
Balance Sheet
December 31, 2017

ASSETS			LIABILITIES		
Current assets			**Current liabilities**		
Cash	$	2,100	Notes payable	$	5,000
Petty cash		100	Accounts payable		35,900
Temporary investments		10,000	Wages payable		8,500
Accounts receivable - net		40,500	Interest payable		2,900
Inventory		31,000	Taxes payable		6,100
Supplies		3,800	Warranty liability		1,100
Prepaid insurance		1,500	Unearned revenues		1,500
Total current assets		89,000	Total current liabilities		61,000
Investments		36,000	**Long-term liabilities**		
			Notes payable		20,000
Property, plant & equipment			Bonds payable		400,000
Land		5,500	Total long-term liabilities		420,000
Land improvements		6,500			
Buildings		180,000			
Equipment		201,000	Total liabilities		481,000
Less: accum depreciation		(56,000)			
Prop, plant & equip - net		337,000			
Intangible assets			**STOCKHOLDERS' EQUITY**		
Goodwill		105,000	Common stock		110,000
Trade names		200,000	Retained earnings		220,000
Total intangible assets		305,000	Accum other comprehensive income		9,000
			Less: Treasury stock		(50,000)
Other assets		3,000	Total stockholders' equity		289,000
Total assets		$ 770,000	Total liabilities & stockholders' equity		$ 770,000

The notes to the sample balance sheet have been omitted.

- Presentation of assets (what is owned), liabilities (what is owed), and the net worth (the difference between the two)

- Captures the picture at the close of business one day in time

18

Income Statement and Net Income

- Presentation of the revenues and expenses for a specific period of time (in contrast to the Balance Sheet)

- Most common are for one quarter, six months, or a year

Example Corporation
Income Statement
For the year ended December 31, 2017

Sales (all on credit)	$500,000
Cost of goods sold	380,000
Gross profit	120,000
Operating expenses	
Selling expenses	35,000
Administrative expenses	45,000
Total operating expenses	80,000
Operating income	40,000
Interest expense	12,000
Income before taxes	28,000
Income tax expense	5,000
Net income after taxes	$ 23,000
Earnings per share	$ 0.23
(based on 100,000 shares outstanding)	

19

19

Statement of Cash Flows

Good Deal Co.
Statement of Cash Flows
For the *Three Months* Ended March 31, 2017

Operating Activities	
Net income	$ 300
Increase in accounts receivable	0
Increase in inventory	(200)
Cash provided (used) in operating activities	100
Investing Activities	0
Financing Activities	
Investment by owner	$2,000
Net increase in cash	2,100
Cash at the beginning of the year	0
Cash at March 31, 2017	$2,100

- In accordance with ASC 230, a Statement of Cash Flows is required in the annual report

- Shows a company's cash receipts and payments during a specific accounting period

- Reflects a reconciliation of cash; does NOT provide a credit view of cash flow

- Non-cash items that may appear: depreciation, amortization, bad debt provision, impairment of goodwill

20

20

Accountant's Notes

Notes to the Financial Statements

1. Many analysts read the Accountant's Notes first

2. Listing of significant points regarding specific balance sheet or income statement accounts that need to be understood when analyzing the other parts of the financial statement

3. Details about a company's leasing activities will appear in the Accountant's Notes, along with in-depth analysis of its debt, assets and other activities

21

Lease Accounting Terms

Residual/ Unguaranteed Residual

The estimated fair market value of the leased property at the end of the lease term

Bargain Purchase Option

A provision allowing the lessee to purchase the leased property at less than the expected fair market value

Fair Market Value

The price that the property could be sold for in an arm's length transaction between unrelated parties

Contingent Rentals

Increases or decreases in lease payments that result from changes occurring subsequent to the inception of the lease in the factors on which lease payments are based

Discount Rate for Lessor

"The interest rate in the deal," states Shawn Halladay, CLFP

Discount Rate for Lessee

Implicit Rate, if known; or, the Lessee Incremental Borrowing Rate: The rate which the lessee could borrow money under the same basic terms and conditions as the lease

22

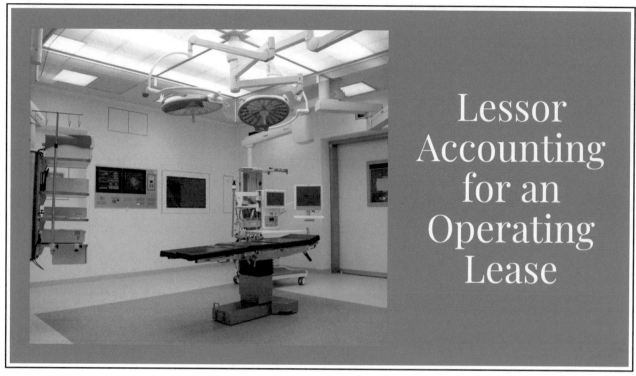

23

Accounting for an Operating Lease

Lease Term	36 months
Number of Lease Payments	36 months (made monthly in advance)
Number of Advance Payments	1
Amount of Monthly Payments	$1,210
Refundable Security Deposit	$6,000
Broker Fees	$0
Cost of Leased Assets	$60,000
Unguaranteed Residual Value	FMV (estimated to be 40%)

24

24

Slide 25

Lessor's Balance Sheet – Assets at Lease Commencement (Operating Lease)

ASSETS

Cash ($1,210 first payment + $6,000 security deposit)	$ 7,210
Leased Equipment	60,000
Less Depreciation	0
TOTAL ASSETS	**$67,210**

Slide 26

Lessor's Balance Sheet – Liabilities and Equity at Lease Commencement (Operating Lease)

LIABILITIES

Security Deposit	$ 6,000
Advance Payment	1,210
Total Liabilities	7,210
EQUITY (NET WORTH)	$60,000
TOTAL LIABILITIES AND EQUITY	$67,210

Slide 27

Lessor's Income Statement at End of 1st Month (Operating Lease)

Lessor's Income Statement at End of First Month - Operating

INCOME		
Rental Income	$ 1,210	
TOTAL INCOME		1,210
EXPENSES		
Depreciation (($60,000-$24,000)/36)	1,000	
TOTAL EXPENSES		(1,000)
NET INCOME		$210

Slide 28

Lessor Accounting for a Sales-Type Lease

Accounting for a Sales-Type Lease

Lease Term	48 months
Number of Lease Payments	48 months (made monthly in advance)
Number of Advance Payments	1
Amount of Monthly Payments	$1,517
Refundable Security Deposit	$1,000
Broker Fees	$0
Cost of Leased Assets	$65,000
Unguaranteed Residual Value	FMV (estimated to be 10%)

29

Lessor's Balance Sheet – Assets at Lease Commencement (Sales-Type Lease)

ASSETS

Cash ($1,517 first payment + $1,000 security deposit)	$ 2,517
Minimum Lease Payments Receivable ($1,517 x 47) 71,299	
Unguaranteed Residual ($65,000 x 10%)	6,500
Unearned Income (($1,517 x 48) + $6,500 - $65,000)	(14,316)
Net Investment in Lease	63,483
TOTAL ASSETS	$66,000

30

Slide 31

Lessor's Balance Sheet – Liabilities and Equity at Lease Commencement (Sales-Type Lease)		
LIABILITIES		
Security Deposit		$ 1,000
Total Liabilities		1,000
EQUITY (NET WORTH)		65,000
TOTAL LIABILITIES AND EQUITY		$66,000

31

Slide 32

Lessor's Income Statement at End of 1st Month (Sales-Type Lease)		
INCOME		
Lease Income (use straight line method ($14,316/48))		$ 298.25
TOTAL INCOME		298.25
EXPENSES		
Depreciation		0
TOTAL EXPENSES		0
NET INCOME		$298.25

32

The Academy for Lease & Finance Professionals

Credit
125 Points
25 Questions

Setting the Standards of Professionalism For Over 30 years

1

The Origination Lifecycle

Sales

Credit

Documentation

Funding

2

2

Sales vs. Credit

Opposite directions, but working toward the same goal.

Sales

- Paid to find fundable transactions
- Accentuate positives
- Help gain as many approvals as possible

Credit

- Determine acceptability of a deal based on inherent risk and credit policy
- Be cautious, require clarity and transparency
- Assess risk
- Evaluate the deal in relation to the overall portfolio

3

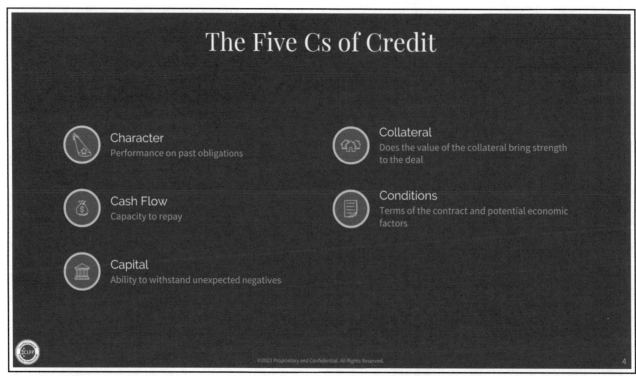

The Five Cs of Credit

Character
Performance on past obligations

Collateral
Does the value of the collateral bring strength to the deal

Cash Flow
Capacity to repay

Conditions
Terms of the contract and potential economic factors

Capital
Ability to withstand unexpected negatives

4

Risk Appetite Framework

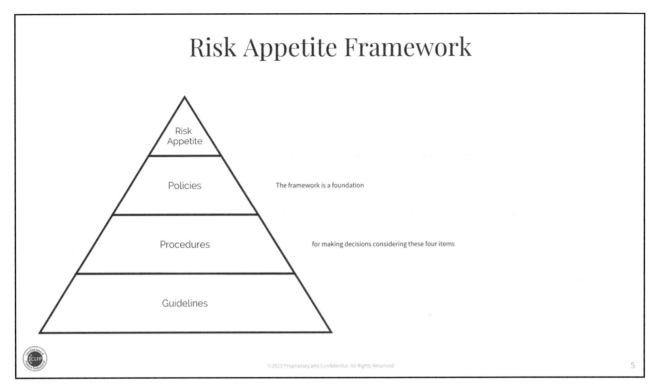

The framework is a foundation

for making decisions considering these four items

5

5

Expected Loss

For banks, every large credit decision must have a probability of default ("PD") and loss given default ("LGD") risk rating as part of the credit package.
% PD x LGD x EAD = Expected Loss

- PD: Probability of default provides an estimate of the likelihood that a borrower will be unable to repay debt obligations

- LGD: Loss given default refers to the amount of money a bank or other financial institution would lose should a borrower default on a loan

- EAD: Exposure at default

6

6

Credit Process

| Credit Request/Credit Application | Data Gathering and Due Diligence | Credit Analysis | Credit Decision |

7

Variations by Transaction Size

Each company may define these ranges slightly differently, but the size of the transaction has an effect on the credit valuation and decision.

Small-Ticket

Transactions under $250,000

May use auto-decision

Mid-Ticket

Transactions under $5,000,000

Takes into account the small-ticket aspects, but often financial statements and in some cases, bank or trade references are required

Large-Ticket

Transactions over $5,000,000

Takes into account the small- and mid-ticket requirements, but also may include reviewing public information, bank agreements with covenants and projections.

8

Due Diligence

- When it comes to "due diligence," how much diligence is due?
  The level of due diligence for a credit evaluation will vary based on the origination channel, the size of the transaction, and the risk appetite framework of the lessor/lender

9

9

Know the Origination Channel

- ### Direct Origination
  Lender to end-user

- ### TPO
  Lender to broker to end-user

- ### Vendor
  Lender to manufacturer/dealer to end-user

10

KYC – Know Your Customer

Company's Growth

- You must understand the entity that is being granted credit

- Accurately identify the owners of the business

- Delicate balance between due diligence vs. cost vs. risk

- Requirements might be less stringent for non-regulated lessors

- Background checks are critical in ensuring the lender is not aiding in terrorist or illegal activity

- Fraud prevention

- Know the legal entity (Corp, LLC, Sole Prop, etc.)

11

11

Know the Legal Entity

- Sole Proprietor

- Partnerships

- Corporations

- Other variations

12

12

Sole Proprietorship

- Individual(s) operating with a trade name - sometimes called a "DBA"

- Does not require a filing with State or Federal government in order to exist

- Is not insulated from liability (he/she can be sued for company debts)

13

13

Sole Proprietorship

1. No legal requirements to start the business outside normal business licenses and specific licenses that apply to the industry

2. Owner may sign the contract

3. Only one tax return (individual's Form 1040); equity owners are personally taxed

4. Some states have usury laws applicable to sole proprietors and there are other issues that make dealing with individuals operating under trade names somewhat risky

14

14

Partnerships

- Two or more individuals doing business

- Usually documented via a partnership agreement

- Income and losses are generally taxed directly to the partners rather than at the partnership level

15

15

General and Limited Partnership

General Partnership	Limited Partnership
Two or more individuals, or entities (e.g., corporations, LLC, etc.)	At least one party needs to be the general partner, and others may be limited partners
Each personally liable for all activities of the business	General partners are liable for all activities and liabilities of the business
May be formed without filing with government (some states permit registration)	Limited partners limit their liability to their investment (and any liabilities they personally guarantee)

16

16

Corporations

- A legal entity separate and distinct from its owners (shareholders) and officers in the view of other businesses, the law, and taxing authorities

- Investors are shareholders, either common, preferred, or both, and liability is limited to their investment plus any debts they individually guarantee

- Formed by filing Articles of Incorporation with the Secretary of State

17

17

Key Issues in Dealing with Corporations

Whether a transaction must be approved by a "resolution" of the board of directors

Whether an officer signing a document is who he or she claims to be

Addressed by an incumbency or secretary certificate showing specimen signatures and certifying as to the signer's title

Whether the information obtained about the corporation is accurate and the corporation is in existence and able to transact business

18

18

Types of Corporations

"C" Corporation

This is the basic corporate form

There are no limits to the number of shareholders

Profits are taxed to the corporation itself and distributions to the shareholders are also taxed

"S" Corporation

Elects under specific IRS guidelines to be taxed in the manner of a partnership

The number and types of shareholders are limited by IRS regulations

All profits and losses flow to the individual shareholders and are reflected in the shareholders' tax returns

19

19

Other Corporations

Not-For-Profit Corporation

Entity usually formed to provide some services and whose purpose and motives are not profit-oriented

Non-profits issue their own financial statements and have the legal ability to borrow money

Professional Corporation ("PC")

In most states, individuals in specific professions such as physicians, dentists, and attorneys, may incorporate as a professional corporation

Provides certain tax and pension benefits and limits the individual's personal liability for normal business matters

For the individual shareholder(s) to be liable for the business obligations of the corporation, they must sign a personal guaranty

20

20

Limited Liability Company (LLC)

- LLCs are similar to Sub "S" corporations in that their profits or losses flow through to the owners' ("members") tax returns

- Similar to partnerships in that they are governed by an agreement among the members and do not generally have boards of directors

- Unlike a Sub "S" corporation, the owners may be individuals or corporations, and the number of owners is not limited

21

Limited Liability Company (LLC)

Formed by filing Articles of Organization with the Secretary of State

Governed by Operating Agreements

The terms of these documents govern whether the LLC is managed by one or more managers or by the members directly

It is important to determine who has authority to bind the LLC to equipment finance agreements

No personal liability unless they personally guarantee the debts

22

Other Variations of Business Entities

Joint Venture

- Two or more companies set up a joint venture entity for a specific project or to provide a vehicle to handle a certain type of business in which the creating entities have a common interest
- A separate financial statement is prepared for the entity and the joint venture members share the resulting profits or losses
- Joint ventures are dissolved at some future date

Association

- Used mostly by organizations that are not generally in a commercial enterprise
- Usually non-profit organizations with little if any assets
- Bylaws should be reviewed to ensure that the association has the authority to borrow money and to determine who can commit the association to the indebtedness

Trust

- A trust is formed to hold assets for the benefit of others, such as an equipment trust, to which is assigned certain equipment to be used as collateral for an obligation
- A Trust Agreement shows the name of the trust, identifies the trustee, the responsibility of the trustee, the beneficiary of the trust, and the powers of the trustee
- It is important to review the Trust Agreement before entertaining any type of credit request

23

Strengths of Business Organizations

Sole Proprietor

Owner is the recipient of all profits and losses, taxed as an individual

Low costs to operate and organize

Partnership

Enhanced borrowing and access to capital with multiple owners

Taxed as personal income

Corporation

Limited liability for owners, some tax advantages

Ability to grow and expand

24

Weaknesses of Business Organizations

Sole Proprietor

Owner has unlimited liability and limited access to funds

Business is dissolved upon the death of the proprietor

Partnership

Partners have unlimited liability, and it is difficult to transfer the partnership

Partnership is dissolved upon death of a partner

Corporation

Taxes and expenses are generally higher

More government regulation

25

Entities Summary

	Sole Proprietor	Partnership	Ltd. Partnership	C Corporation	S Corporation	LLC
Minimum Number of Equity Owners	1	2	2	1	1	1
Equity Owners of the business are personally taxed for business' profits	Yes	Yes	Yes	No	Yes	Yes
Lessor can go immediately and directly after equity owners if company defaults on a lease	Yes	Yes	No*	No	No	No
Continues in existence as is if one or more equity owners die	No	No**	Yes	Yes	Yes	Yes

* can go after general partner only
** but partnership agreement might affect this answer

26

Qualification to Do Business

27

Licensing and Being in "Good Standing"

- All states require that foreign corporations (those formed outside the state) "qualify to do business"

  Businesses achieve this by obtaining a Certificate of Authority if the corporation is "doing business" within the state

- In most states, having an office or an agent that regularly transacts business in the state is required to qualify to do business

- In some, merely having a significant number of leases, or other business, or obtaining a sales tax or other registration is enough to require the corporation to qualify to do business

28

28

Foreign Corporation

- A business or legal entity formed under the laws of a different state and doing business in another state must register to do business in a state, if:
  - They have a physical office/place of business
  - There is the presence of an agent, employed by the foreign corporation
  - Routine visits to the state, with a temporary site
  - Pay sales, use or property tax in the state

29

Taxes

- Qualifying to do business as a foreign corporation involves the payment of franchise taxes

- Property taxes are payable for property location irrespective of whether the owner has registered with the Secretary of State or any separate legal entity

  The presence of equipment in a state allows the state to assess property taxes

- Sales and use taxes are payable on equipment purchased or leased in the state

- Income taxes are payable generally wherever a lessor's business generates taxable income

30

Fraud

Fraudulent Financial Statements

Fake Vendor

Forged Documents

No Equipment

31

CECL (Current Expected Credit Loss)

Issued by FASB in 2016

Requirement for all types of lenders to forecast future losses on their current portfolio	Although it is an Accounting standard, each financial institution will implement it differently A cross-functional approach will be needed between the various departments

32

32

Credit Evaluation Tools

- **Credit Scores**
  Personal credit score, business credit score

- **Credit Bureaus**
  Consumer bureaus, business bureaus, D&B PayNet

- **Financial Statement Analysis**
  Ratios, financial spreading software or spreadsheets

- **Non-Traditional Data Sources**
  Social media, internet searches, online reviews, etc.

- **Risk Ratings and Risk Scores**
  Agency ratings (Moodys, S&P, Fitch)
  PG, LGD, Expected Loss

- **Industry Peer Comparison**
  D&B, TROYs, Value Line, IBIS World, RMA

33

Benefits of Credit Scoring & Analysis

- Quicker, cheaper and more objective

- May reduce the time to process an application to minutes

- May reduce the time needed to work through the approval process

- May help lenders comply with Regulation B and other fair lending regulations

34

Scorecard

- Scoring model built by developers

- Historical data is analyzed on previous deals to determine which characteristics predict applicant performance

- Historic portfolio must be of sufficient size to provide a statistically valid sample of deals

  Need a sample of both good (non-default) and bad (default) transactions

35

Financial Ratios

↑ Increasing ratios that reflect positive trends:	↓ Decreasing ratios that reflect positive trends:
• Return on Sales (Gross Profit Margin)	• Accounts Receivable Turnover in Days
• Net Profit Margin	• Inventory Turnover in Days
• Current Ratio	• Accounts Payable Turnover in Days
• Quick Ratio	• Total Liabilities to Net Worth

The following ratios cannot be viewed by themselves, as either positive or negative: Return on Assets and Return on Equity.

- Compare the results of the company being analyzed against results from calculating the same ratios in prior years to determine any trends in financial performance

- Compare the results of the company being analyzed against the same ratios computed for its industry peers to determine if the company's financial performance is better or worse than its industry peers

- Trend analysis

36

Financial Ratios

Profitability Ratios

Gross Profit Margin

Operating Profit Margin

Net Profit Margin

Return on Assets

Return on Equity

Liquidity Ratios

Current Ratio

Quick Ratio

Accounts Receivable Turnover

Inventory Turnover

Accounts Payable Turnover

Leverage Ratios

Total Liabilities to Net Worth

Debt to EBITDA

Long Term Debt to Capitalization

37

37

Gross Profit Margin

$$\frac{\textit{Gross Profit on Sales}}{\textit{Net Sales}}$$

- Result of the cost of goods sold subtracted from net sales after returns and allowances

- Steady or increasing trends are positive

- Declines need specific justification

38

38

Return on Equity

- Ratio of net profit, after taxes and/or S corporation distributions, divided by net worth

- Especially with Sub S and closely held corporations, net profits after taxes and distributions may be artificially low

  Some shareholders take out large distributions and then lend the funds back to the corporation

- A steady to increasing percentage is positive

$$\frac{Net\ Income\ (after\ taxes)}{Net\ Worth}$$

39

Current Ratio

$$\frac{Current\ Assets}{Current\ Liabilities}$$

- Current Ratio is a general gauge of a company's ability to meet short term liabilities coming due in the next operating period

- The higher the better, but generally a ratio of more than 1:1 is preferred

40

Quick Ratio

- Also known as the "Acid Test"

- A ratio over 1:1 is good and a better indicator of a company's ability to pay its current liabilities than the Current Ratio

$$\frac{Quick\ assets\ (current\ assets\ -\ inventory)}{Current\ Liabilities}$$

41

Inventory Turnover

$$\frac{Average\ Inventory}{Cost\ of\ Goods\ Sold} * 365 = Days$$

- The inventory turn over formula yields the number of days inventory turns over in one accounting period

- Valuable ratio for spotting understocking, overstocking, obsolescence, and need for merchandising improvement

- Remember that turnover ratios are improving if they are decreasing

42

Debt to Equity

- Relationship of borrowed funds compared with owners' capital

- An increasing trend may suggest a leverage problem

$$\frac{Total\ Liabilities}{Net\ Worth\ (owners'equity)},$$

43

Debt to EBITDA

EBITDA - Earnings before interest, tax, depreciation and amortization

$$\frac{Liabilities}{EBITDA}$$

- Measurement of a company's ability to pay its debts

- Differing views on what should be included

- Conservative approach would be to include all debt

44

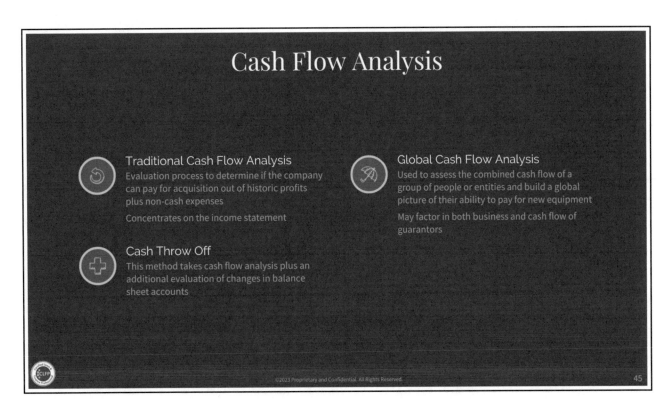

Cash Flow Analysis

Traditional Cash Flow Analysis
Evaluation process to determine if the company can pay for acquisition out of historic profits plus non-cash expenses

Concentrates on the income statement

Cash Throw Off
This method takes cash flow analysis plus an additional evaluation of changes in balance sheet accounts

Global Cash Flow Analysis
Used to assess the combined cash flow of a group of people or entities and build a global picture of their ability to pay for new equipment

May factor in both business and cash flow of guarantors

45

45

Trend Analysis

Analysts should evaluate trends over a three- or four-year period

- Increasing ratios that reflect positive trends
  - Return on Sales
  - Net Profit Margin
  - Current Ratio
  - Quick Ratio

- Decreasing ratios that reflect positive trends
  - Accounts Receivable Turnover in Days
  - Inventory Turnover in Days
  - Accounts Payable Turnover in Days
  - Total Liabilities to Net Worth

46

46

Industry Review and Comparison

- RMA

  Industry average tables prepared by the Risk Management Association

  Data is from businesses that have relationships with commercial banks

- NAICS

  The North American Industry Classification System

  Standard used by federal statistical agencies in classifying business establishments for the purpose of collecting, analyzing and publishing statistical data related to the U.S. economy

  Compare with industry standards such as: gross profit margin, typical net profit margin, and typical receivable turnover

47

The Academy for Lease & Finance Professionals

Pricing
100 Points
30 Questions

1

The Time Value of Money

A $1.00 received today is worth more than $1.00 received one year from today because of the ability of that $1.00 to earn something over the next year.

2

2

"Time Zero"

- Time Zero (T0) is also known as the time of Present Value (PV)

- In a lease or equipment finance agreement, T0 is the Transaction Date

  Any equipment is funded

  Any security deposit is paid by customer

  Any advance payments are made by customer

3

"Time Zero"
Continued

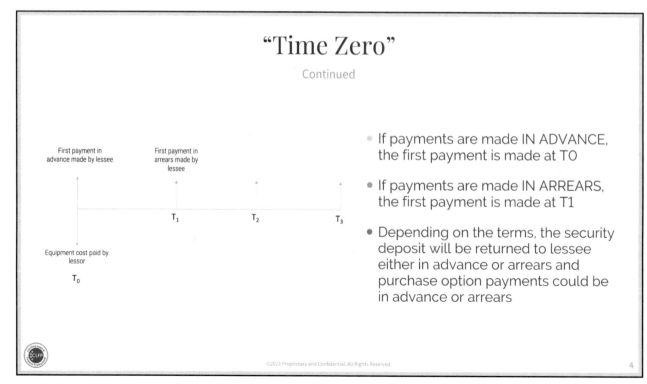

- If payments are made IN ADVANCE, the first payment is made at T0

- If payments are made IN ARREARS, the first payment is made at T1

- Depending on the terms, the security deposit will be returned to lessee either in advance or arrears and purchase option payments could be in advance or arrears

4

The Time Value of Money

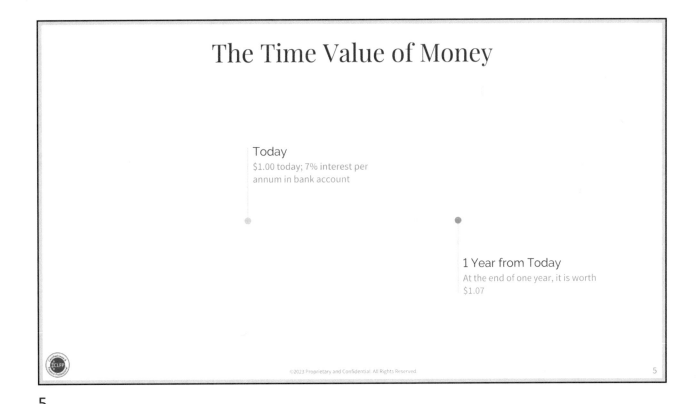

Today
$1.00 today; 7% interest per annum in bank account

1 Year from Today
At the end of one year, it is worth $1.07

5

The Time Value of Money

- Calculation:

RESID (FV)	=	Solve for
I%	=	7% per annum
TERM	=	12 months (1 year)
LEASE	=	$1.00

- Future Value =
$1.07

Compounding Period: Monthly			Nominal Annual Rate: 7.000 %	
	EVENT	DATE	AMOUNT	NUMBER
1	Lease	01/01/2023	100.00	1
2	Residual	01/01/2024	107.23	1

6

6

The Time Value of Money
Discounting

Today
The amount that dollar is worth must be "discounted" by 7% to determine what its value is today = $.93

1 year from now
If $1.00 is paid a year from now, the ability to earn the 7% interest has been taken away

7

7

The Time Value of Money
Discounting Example

- Calculation:

RESID (FV)	=	$1.00
I%	=	7% per annum
TERM	=	12 months (1 year)
LEASE	=	Solve for

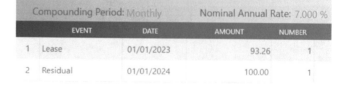

	EVENT	DATE	AMOUNT	NUMBER
Compounding Period: Monthly			Nominal Annual Rate: 7.000 %	
1	Lease	01/01/2023	93.26	1
2	Residual	01/01/2024	100.00	1

- Lease = $.9326

8

8

Things to Keep in Mind...

- For all slides – when using TValue and there are zero payments in advance, you need to adjust the residual to be collected on the same date as the end of the stream of payments

- The calculator formula provided will automatically adjust for it

9

9

What if we are to receive $12, in monthly payments of $1.00 each over the next year (in arrears). What would the $12 be worth today, considering a discount rate of 6%?

- TERM = 12

- I% = 6%

- PMT = $1.00

- RESID = $0.00

- LEASE = Solve for

- LEASE (PV) = $11.62

Compounding Period: Monthly		Nominal Annual Rate: 6.000 %		>>	Label:
EVENT	DATE	AMOUNT	NUMBER	PERIOD	END DATE
1 Lease	01/01/2023	11.62	1		
2 Lease Payment	02/01/2023	1.00	12	Monthly	01/01/2024

10

10

Terminology

Yield
Total value of all cash flows stated as an annual percentage rate

Implicit Rate
Value of rent (or payments) and residual stated as an annual percentage rate

Running Rate or Stream Rate
Value of rent stated as an annual percentage rate without consideration of other factors (residual) that affect the actual interest rate

Lease Rate or Lease Rate Factor
Monthly payment stated as a percentage of the original equipment cost

11

Terminology

Discount Rate
Interest rate used when discounting a series of payments to the present value

Internal Rate of Return
Interest rate that makes the present value of the cash flow(s) equal to the investment (i.e. equipment cost or loan amount)

Points
Term that refers to the percentage of profit or commission that is "priced in" or "to be paid" to the broker, originator or seller of a transaction

Basis Point
One-hundredth of 1; is usually used when discussing differences in interest rates

12

Calculating Present Value

Major Variables

Term (N)/(Period)

Rate (I%)/(Nominal Annual Rate)

Present Value (PV)/(Lease)

Payment (PMT)/(Amount)

Future Value (FV)(Residual)

Minor Variables

Advance Payments (#ADV)

Fees Paid Out (FEE)

Fees Received (CLOSFEE)

Security Deposit (SECDEP)

13

13

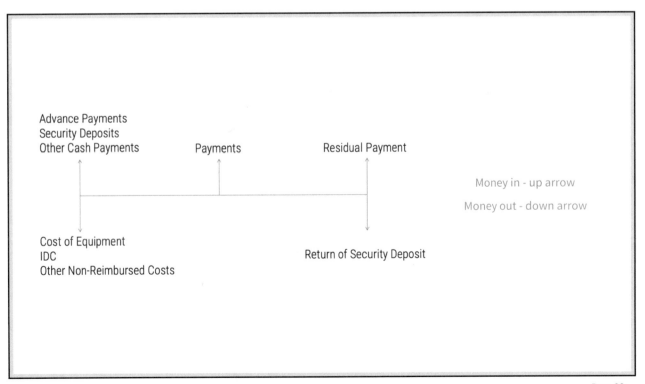

14

Rate Factor

Non-Tax Pricing

- The Rate Factor is that number, that when multiplied with the cost of the equipment, will give the periodic payment amount

- The factor is expressed as the periodic payment amount for an equipment cost of $1.00

- Factor x Equipment Cost = Payment

- Payment/Equipment Cost = Factor

- Payment/Factor = Equipment Cost

15

15

Rate Factor Example

- Term = 36 months

- Advance Payments = 2

- Rate = 18%

- Payment
  Solve for (this will be your rate factor)

- Hint:
  If using a calculator, use $1 for LEASE and $0 for RESID

  If using TValue, use $1,000 for PV/Equipment Cost and $0 for Residual and divide by 1,000

- Rate Factor = .0351

16

16

- Term = 60
- Rate = 15%
- Equipment cost = $185,000
- Residual = $18,500
- # of Advance payments = 0
- IDC = $0
- Security deposit = $0
- Other fees = $0
- Payment = Solve for

Warmup Problem

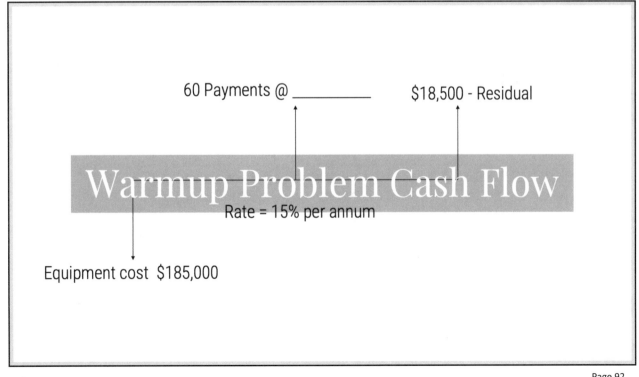

60 Payments @ _____ $18,500 - Residual

Warmup Problem Cash Flow

Rate = 15% per annum

Equipment cost $185,000

Warmup Problem TValue Entries

Compounding Period: Monthly		Nominal Annual Rate: 15.000 %			>>	Label:
EVENT	**DATE**	**AMOUNT**	**NUMBER**	**PERIOD**		**END DATE**
1 Lease	01/01/2023	185,000.00	1			
2 Lease Payment	02/01/2023	Unknown	60	Monthly		01/01/2028
3 Residual	01/01/2028	18,500.00	1			

19

Warmup Problem Answer

- $4,192.27

- Rate Factor:
  $4,192.27/$185,000 = .02266

20

20

Effects of Down and Advance Payments

Down Payments

Reduces the total finance amount

The value entered as the PV will be the Total Equipment Cost minus the Down Payment

Advance Payments

One or more lease payments required to be paid to the lessor at the beginning of the lease term

Typically first and last

The more payments that are "moved" from the end of the payment schedule to the beginning, the more the yield increases

21

Effects of Residual Values/End of Term Payments and Security Deposits

Residual Value/End of Term Payments

Payment due at the end of the contract such as a fixed buyout, residual payment (if lease) or balloon payment (if loan)

Security Deposit

Additional amount that may be required in place of, or in addition to, advanced payments

May be necessary to enhance the yield of a transaction, to help mitigate risk of the transaction, or both

22

Unusual Payment Structures

Delayed Payments

At the beginning of the contract, no payments are required for a period of time

Step Payments

Payment(s) increase (step-up) or decrease (step-down) in size during the term of the lease

Hi-Low Payments

Payments start high and lower over the term of the contract.

Contact Payments

A lower payment (usually $100 or so) is made each month for a period

Keeps the customer in the habit of receiving and paying invoices for the contract

Seasonal Payments

Payments structured so that there are no payments made for a specific period of time each year (usually several months) to coincide with the businesses cash flow

23

Lease Pricing Tools

Most unusual payment structures are too difficult and complicated to compute using a financial calculator. They are best calculated using various pricing programs such as the following:

Financial Calculator

Used to calculate any of the five major variables of lease pricing for a constant stream of payments and with customized formulas you can program the financial calculator to include the minor variables as well

SuperTRUMP and InfoAnalysis

Used for tax-based pricing and complex pricing

TValue

Used for small-ticket, structured, non-tax pricing scenarios

Custom Spreadsheet (Microsoft Excel)

Formulas may be used to create customized pricing

24

True (Tax) Lease Pricing

Transactions classified as a true tax lease must also integrate the effects of the tax benefits into their lease pricing

Non-tax lease

The lessor recognizes the interest portion of the lease payment as interest income

True tax lease

The lessor recognizes the full amount of the lease payments as rental income, but is also entitled to recognize the depreciation expense of owning the equipment

25

Elements Affecting True (Tax) Lease Pricing

1. Federal income tax rate of the lessor

2. State income tax rate of the lessor

3. Local income tax rate of the lessor

4. Federal MACRS depreciation term for the equipment

5. Lessor's state's treatment of depreciation

6. Lessor's amortizable fees (e.g., doc fees, etc.)

26

Example #1

Term = 60

Rate = 14%

Equipment cost = $100,000

Residual = 5%

# of Advance payments = 0

Broker Fee = 3%

Security Deposit = $0

Other Fees = $0

Payment = Solve for

60 Payments @ $_____   Residual = $5,000

Rate = 14%

Equip cost = $100,000
Broker fee = $ 3,000
TOTAL   = $103,000

27

Example #1 - Entries

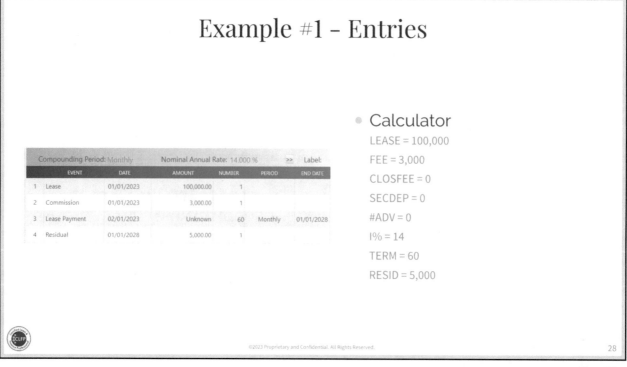

Compounding Period: Monthly		Nominal Annual Rate: 14.000 %		>>	Label:
EVENT	**DATE**	**AMOUNT**	**NUMBER**	**PERIOD**	**END DATE**
1 Lease	01/01/2023	100,000.00	1		
2 Commission	01/01/2023	3,000.00	1		
3 Lease Payment	02/01/2023	Unknown	60	Monthly	01/01/2028
4 Residual	01/01/2028	5,000.00	1		

- Calculator
  LEASE = 100,000
  FEE = 3,000
  CLOSFEE = 0
  SECDEP = 0
  #ADV = 0
  I% = 14
  TERM = 60
  RESID = 5,000

28

28

Slide 29

Example #1 Answer

Payment = $2,338.62

29

Slide 30

48 Payments @ $_____   Residual $11,250

Rate = 12.5%

Equipment cost	$75,000
Broker fee	$2,625
TOTAL	$77,625

Example #2

Term = 48

Rate = 12.5%

Equipment Cost = $75,000

Residual = 15%

# of Advance Payments = 0

Broker Fee = 3.5%

Other Fees = $0

Payment = Solve For

30

Example #2 – Entries

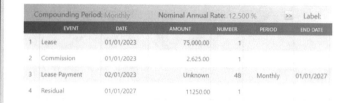

	EVENT	DATE	AMOUNT	NUMBER	PERIOD	END DATE
1	Lease	01/01/2023	75,000.00	1		
2	Commission	01/01/2023	2,625.00	1		
3	Lease Payment	02/01/2023	Unknown	48	Monthly	01/01/2027
4	Residual	01/01/2027	11250.00	1		

Compounding Period: Monthly   Nominal Annual Rate: 12.500 %   >>   Label:

- Calculator
  LEASE = 75,000
  FEE = 2,625
  CLOSFEE = 0
  SECDEP = 0
  #ADV = 0
  I% = 12.5%
  TERM = 48
  RESID = 11,250

31

31

Example #2 Answer

Payment = $1,881.43

32

32

Slide 33

Example #3

Term = 42

Rate = 18%

Equipment cost = $120,000

Residual = 10%

# of Advance payments = 4

Broker Fee = 3%

Security Deposit = 20%

Other Fees = $0

Payment = Solve for

Security deposit $24,000   38 Payments @
1 Payment $_____ $_____   Residual $12,000

                                          3 Payments @ $0

                                   Rate = 18%

Equipment cost $120,000
Broker fee $ 3,600   Security deposit $24,000
TOTAL $123,600

33

Slide 34

Example #3 - Entries

Compounding Period: Monthly		Nominal Annual Rate: 18.000 %		>>	Label:
EVENT	**DATE**	**AMOUNT**	**NUMBER**	**PERIOD**	**END DATE**
1 Lease	01/01/2023	120,000.00	1		
2 Commission	01/01/2023	3,600.00	1		
3 Security Deposit	01/01/2023	24,000.00	1		
4 Lease Payment	01/01/2023	4.000x	1		
5 Lease Payment	02/01/2023	Unknown	38	Monthly	03/01/2026
6 Lease Payment	04/01/2026	0.00	3	Monthly	06/01/2026
7 Residual	07/01/2026	12,000.00	1		
8 Return Sec Dep	07/01/2026	24,000.00	1		

- Calculator

  LEASE = 120,000

  FEE = 3,600

  CLOSFEE = 0

  SECDEP = 24,000

  #ADV = 4

  I% = 18

  TERM = 42

  RESID = 12,000

34

34

Example #3 Answer
Payment = $3,231.85

35

$10,505

46 Payments @ $5,252.50

1 @ $64,500

1 @ $0

Rate = 14%

Equipment cost $_____

Example #4

Term = 48

Rate = 14%

Equipment Cost = Solve for

Residual = $64,500

# of Advance Payments = 2

Security Deposit = $0

Broker Fee = 0%

Other Fees = $0

Payment = $5,252.50

36

Example #4 - Entries

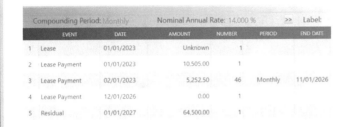

	EVENT	DATE	AMOUNT	NUMBER	PERIOD	END DATE
	Compounding Period: Monthly		Nominal Annual Rate: 14.000 %		>>	Label:
1	Lease	01/01/2023	Unknown	1		
2	Lease Payment	01/01/2023	10,505.00	1		
3	Lease Payment	02/01/2023	5,252.50	46	Monthly	11/01/2026
4	Lease Payment	12/01/2026	0.00	1		
5	Residual	01/01/2027	64,500.00	1		

- Calculator
  - FEE = 0
  - CLOSFEE = 0
  - SECDEP = 0
  - #ADV = 2
  - PMT = 5252.50
  - I% = 14%
  - TERM = 48
  - RESID = 64,500

37

Example #4 Answer

Equipment Cost = $233,625.32

38

Term = 60

Rate = Solve for

Equipment cost = $225,000

Residual = 10%

# of Advance payments = 3

Broker Fee = 2%

Security Deposit = 10%

Other Fees = $0

Payment = $5,206.50

Example #5

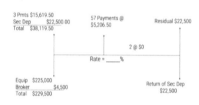

39

Example #5 - Entries

	EVENT	DATE	AMOUNT	NUMBER	PERIOD	END DATE
	Compounding Period: Monthly		Nominal Annual Rate: Unknown	>>	Label:	
1	Lease	01/01/2023	225,000.00	1		
2	Commission	01/01/2023	4,500.00	1		
3	Security Deposit	01/01/2023	22,500.00	1		
4	Lease Payment	01/01/2023	15,619.50	1		
5	Lease Payment	02/01/2023	5,206.50	57	Monthly	10/01/2027
6	Lease Payment	11/01/2027	0.00	2	Monthly	12/01/2027
7	Return Sec Dep	01/01/2028	22,500.00	1		
8	Residual	01/01/2028	22,500.00	1		

+ Click here to add a new line

- Calculator

LEASE = 225,000

FEE = 4,500

CLOSFEE = 0

SECDEP = 22,500

#ADV = 3

PMT = 5206.50

TERM = 60

RESID = 22,500

40

40

Example #5 Answer
Rate = 19.804%

The Academy for Lease & Finance Professionals

Setting the Standards of Professionalism For Over 30 years

Documentation

125 points

39 Questions

1

Lease Agreements

Standard/"One-off" Lease Agreement	Master Lease Agreement	Plain Language ("Plain English") Agreement
Lease governing only one transaction	Single document under which a lessee may add additional schedules representing property later acquired, subject to the same general terms and conditions	Lease documents that have been edited for purposes of making them shorter and more easily understood, avoiding "legalese"

2

2

Standard Documents

3

Standard Documents

Lease Contract

Lessor agrees to provide equipment or other personal property or rights to a lessee in return for rental payments

Lease Schedule

Documents used with Master Leases; not to be confused with exhibit-type Schedules

Guaranty

Contains all credit support provided by third parties that are not primary lessees

It is a guarantee of performance; not collection

UCC Filing

Filed in the Office of the Secretary of State where the lessee is incorporated

4

4

Standard Documents

<table>
<tr>
<td>

"D&A" or Acceptance Certificate

Signed by the lessee, indicating lessee has unconditionally accepted equipment

Date on this document, if any, should be after the date the lease is signed and that the lessee has in fact signed after receiving the equipment

</td>
<td>

Corporate Resolution

In order for a registered entity such as a corporation to enter into a contract outside the "ordinary course of business," the signing individual must be authorized to do so

Certification by the Secretary or other Officer that the person signing is so authorized

Protects the lessor from the lessee raising a defense that the lease is unenforceable because it was executed without the authority or permission of the lessee

</td>
<td>

Exhibits & Schedules

Formal additions to the lease

Not to be confused with Schedules to Master Leases

Examples of when they may be used:

If the description of the leased property is too long

Additional terms or provisions requiring additional space

</td>
</tr>
</table>

5

5

Standard Documents

Landlord/Real Estate Waiver

Document in which landlord acknowledges that certain property on its tenant's premises is owned by the lessor and is leased to the tenant

Landlord agrees to recognize and not interfere with the lessor's rights respecting the lessor's property

Should be signed by the owner of the real property and the lessor

Fixture Filing

Filing similar to a UCC Financing Statement

Recorded by the county recorder of real property records

6

6

Standard Documents

Invoice

The vendor issues the invoice to the lessor seeking payment for the equipment

Demonstrates the passage of title from vendor to lessor

Purchase Order

Issued by a lessor indicating the lessor intends to purchase the equipment from the vendor upon fulfillment of certain conditions by the vendor or lessee

7

7

Standard Documents

Advance Funding/Prefunding Agreement

Describe terms and conditions under which a lessor may advance part or all of the equipment cost to a vendor before full delivery and acceptance of the equipment

Sometimes referred to as a Pre-delivery Hell or High Water Agreement

Purchase Option

May be contained in a lease or as a separate agreement

Addresses the option of the lessee to acquire ownership of the equipment at the end of the lease

8

8

Elements and Provisions
of a Lease Contract

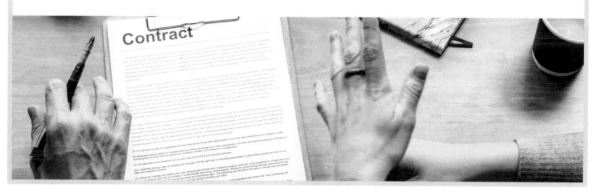

9

Identification of Parties

Supplier of the Equipment (Vendor)

Legal name of the supplier with complete address

Partial satisfaction of Article 2A requirements

Lessee/Lessor

Parties must be specifically identified by correct legal names

Important to get exact names of entities such as corporations, LLCs and other registered organizations exactly the same as their filed names

Creates legally binding contract

Assures accuracy of UCC Financing Statements

10

10

Equipment Description and Location

Complete description of equipment, including serial numbers and quantities

Location identifies proper jurisdiction for sales and property tax purposes

11

Terms

Payment

Correct amount, number and frequency of lease payments

Either state "plus applicable taxes" or state tax amount separately

Purpose/Intent of Agreement

Should state that lessee is paying rent to lessor in return for possession and use of the equipment

State that parties intend transaction to be a lease and not a loan (if true)

Acceptance

Lessee accepts the equipment when fully delivered and operational, after which time the lease is in full effect

12

12

Disclaimer of Warranties

① Lessor makes no warranties as to the condition of the equipment, its merchantability, or its fitness

② Lessee has fully inspected the equipment and the equipment is in good and satisfactory condition

③ Leased equipment is solely for business or commercial purposes (not personal)

④ Lessee leases the equipment "as is" and with all faults

13

13

Disclaimer of Warranties
Continued

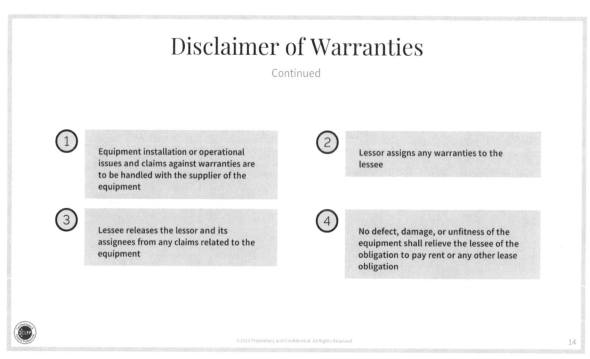

① Equipment installation or operational issues and claims against warranties are to be handled with the supplier of the equipment

② Lessor assigns any warranties to the lessee

③ Lessee releases the lessor and its assignees from any claims related to the equipment

④ No defect, damage, or unfitness of the equipment shall relieve the lessee of the obligation to pay rent or any other lease obligation

14

14

Article 2a (10 in California)

- Clearly distinguishes between the supplier of the equipment and the funder as two separate entities

- Used to guard against "Agency"

  Ensures an arm's length transaction (no partnership)

  Won't compromise legal protections of your documentation

  Can't stop paying due to equipment malfunction

15

15

Assignment of Lease

- Prohibits assignment by lessees to unknown entities or requires lessor's consent

- Allows lessor to discount a lease to a funding source when paired with the Notice and Acknowledgement of Assignment

16

16

Provisions

Rental Commencement and Other Payments

Often links to equipment delivery date and should specify the date first and when remaining payments are due

Verbal verification call is commonly used to confirm the actual due date

Non-Cancellation

The lease may not be cancelled unless the lessor agrees in writing

"Time is of the Essence"

Some state courts still look for this language to indicate that it is expected and part of the contract that all payments and other performance must be completed in a timely manner

Typical wording may include, "Time is of the essence of this lease and acceptance on occasion of late payments or performance shall not be deemed to waive this provision"

17

17

Lessee/Lessor Signatures

May be written or electronic

INCUMBENCY CERTIFICATE

I, _____ , Secretary of _____
do hereby affirm and verify that the duly constituted officers of the Corporation as of
_____ , (year), are :

_____ , President
_____ , Vice President
_____ , Treasurer
_____ , Secretary

A True Record:

Attest:

_____

An incumbency certificate signed by another lessee officer and a copy of the Corporate Resolution are often used to verify the identity and authority of the person signing on behalf of the lessee

18

18

eSignatures

- **Authentication**
  Email Authentication

  Passcode

  Knowledge-Based
  Questions

- **Signature**
  Document may be tagged
  with the signers
  information and places
  where they need to be
  signed and/or initialed

- **Vaulting**
  Method for ensuring that
  you are transferring the
  "authoritative copy" of
  the true original document

19

Choice of Law

- States that the
  law of the state
  where the
  lessor is located
  should govern
  the transaction

- As a general
  rule, the courts
  will uphold the
  Choice of Law if
  the transaction
  bears some
  "reasonable
  relation" to the
  state whose law
  is chosen

20

Security Deposit

- Should state the amount

- Terms of the refund

- How it may be used in case of default

- May be held in an account and commingle with lessor's other assets

21

21

Authorizations, Power of Attorney, Amendments

- Many leases and EFAs state that the lessor/lender may file UCCs without the signature of the lessee/borrower

- Power of Attorney allows the lessor to act as attorney for the lessee for specified actions (e.g., modification of payments if cost of equipment changes)

22

22

Location and Use of Equipment

Location

- Very important for tracking and tax purposes
- Movement without notice to or consent should be prohibited

Use

- The equipment should be used only by the lessee and that such use must at all times be in conformance with the provisions and applicable law

23

23

Renewals

- Most renewal clauses give the lessee the option to extend the term of the lease

- Evergreen Clause/Automatic Renewal

  The lease term is extended month-to-month or longer if the lessee fails to return the equipment

  In other leases, the failure of the lessee to notify the lessor of its intention to return the equipment results in a longer renewal period

  Often under legal scrutiny

24

24

Insurance Requirements

Lessee typically is required to carry property insurance (comprehensive all-risk)

Policy names lessor as loss payee

Loss and damage provision often requires that the lessor be fully compensated for the value of the equipment, but also the income obtained from its use

Liability insurance includes lessor as additional insured

25

25

Liens and Tax Liability

- Equipment should be kept lien-free at all times

- Lessee is responsible for any and all taxes of any kind for the equipment

  Often includes personal property tax which can be very expensive

26

26

Lessee Indemnification of Lessor

- Lessee will indemnify (compensate for damage or loss) and hold lessor fully harmless from and against any claim made regarding the equipment

- Protects the lessor against any claim during or after the term of the lease

Service Charges/Late Fees, Interest

- Common to allow for a short grace period following the due date of a payment, after which a service charge/late fee is imposed

- Must be reasonable and related to additional costs and servicing

  If deemed unreasonable, may be found as a "penalty" and unenforceable

  If deemed to be an "interest charge," it could void the entire lease

  If reasonable, the lessor should be entitled to charge interest on the amounts not received☐

Acts of Default

1. Failure to pay rent when due

2. Failure to pay any other sum due (insurance, taxes, etc.)

3. Breach of any representation or warranty

4. Failure to perform act or obligation under lease

5. Lessee made any false or misleading statements with application

6. Levy, seizure or attachment of equipment

7. Bankruptcy

8. Material, adverse change in condition or financial strength of lessee or guarantor

---

Remedies

- Provides for the lessor's rights in the event of a lessee's default

- Typically includes the following, with language that they are "cumulative"

  Return equipment

  Cancellation or termination of the lease

  Acceleration of all future rentals (Acceleration Clause)

  Payment of damages by formula (PV of future rental payments, PV of residual, etc.)

Waiver of Defense Clause

- Lessee agrees to pay all rent and other obligations directly to any Assignee of the lessor

- Any defenses to collection must be asserted against only the original lessor and not the manufacturer, vendor, or any subsequent assignee

- Most funding sources, syndicators and securitizations will insist on this

31

31

Clauses

Cross-Default Clause	Severability
If lessee has multiple lease agreements, a default under one lease is deemed a default under any or all of the other leases	States that if any provision of the lease is unenforceable under state law, or found by a court to be so, all other provisions of the lease are to be enforced Helps avoid the danger of an entire lease being found to be unenforceable just because one provision was viewed to be improper by a court of law
Hell or High-Water Clause	**Tax Indemnity**
Lessee must make payments even if equipment is lost, confiscated or destroyed The lease is non-cancelable and not subject to setoff, counterclaim or defenses by the lessee	Lessee agrees to pay lessor for any loss of income benefits from any act resulting in the recapture of tax benefits to the lessor

32

32

Additional Collateral

- May be used to enhance an applicant's credit risk or when equipment is highly related to the additional collateral

- May be used to guarantee performance of the lease contract

- Real Estate as Additional Collateral

  Mortgage or Deed of Trust required

  File appropriate documentation with the county in which the real estate is located

33

33

Equipment Finance Agreements (EFAs)

- Loan document that:

  Creates indebtedness on the part of the customer (Borrower, rather than Lessee)

  Creates a security interest in favor of the creditor (Lender, rather than a Lessor)

- Similar to a lease intended as security

  Each payment consists of a principal repayment and interest component

34

34

EFAs vs. Leases

- EFA lender is unlikely to face liability to third parties injured by the equipment because the lender does not own it

- EFA lender does not have tax implications related to the purchase of the equipment or filing of property taxes

- Because interest is charged (whether part of the periodic payment or separately stated), EFAs are likely subject to usury law and other legal interest rate limitations

35

35

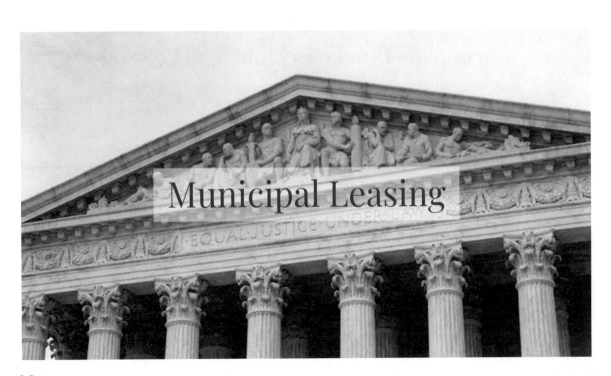

Municipal Leasing

36

Municipal Leasing Documentation

- Non-Appropriation/Fiscal Funding/Annual-Out Clause

  It is unlawful for a currently serving government to obligate funds to be expended after the end of the current fiscal year for which such funds have been budgeted or "appropriated"

  Standard provision that the contract may be terminated without penalty if funds are not appropriated for a particular fiscal period during its term

- The IRS provides that "to be tax-exempt," the agreement must have a dollar purchase option

37

Documents Unique to Municipal Leasing

Certificate of Incumbency/Authority to Sign Lease

Same purpose as a Corporate Secretary's Certificate/Corporate Resolution to Lease

UCC-1

The latest version of the UCC states that the filing of Form UCC-1 does not apply to governmental entities (more than 40 states adopted this)

Certificate of Essential Use

A separate certificate stating the equipment is essential to the lessee

38

Bank Qualification Statement/Form 8038

Bank Qualification Statement

TRA '86 provided that muni interest would remain exempt from federal income tax except for interest received from a large issuer by a commercial bank

"Large Issuer" is one that issues more than $10 million in tax-exempt obligations in the current calendar year

States that the lessee does not "reasonably expect" to issue $10 million+ of tax-exempt obligations and if it does, it will designate the subject lease as being within the "allowable" amount of tax-exempt debt

Form 8038

TRA '86 also provided that munis that lease equipment under tax-exempt leases should file information returns on this form

Form 8038-G is for transactions over $100,000

8038-GC is for aggregate of leases under $100,000

39

Agricultural Leasing

40

Agricultural Leasing Documentation

 Similar to standard leases, but typically more fixed assets

Severance agreements and fixture filings are often necessary

 Added levels of due diligence is necessary due to sales tax implications

A Sales Tax Exemption form is typically part of the document package

③ The increase in technology has led to a common practice where new equipment is attached to existing equipment (e.g., GPS on a tractor that is already owned)

Additional collateral is often required in the credit process

41

Agricultural Leasing Nuances

- Organizational Structures

  There are multiple variations in operating structures for farms

  UCC searches will likely be run on multiple people or entities

- Payment Schedules

  Transactions are not typically monthly; more often annual or semi-annual payments are requested

42

The Academy for Lease & Finance Professionals

Setting the Standards of Professionalism For Over 30 years

Funding, Customer Service and Operations

75 Points

26 Questions

1

Common Methods of Funding/Sources of Capital

- Internal Funding

- Brokering

- Discounting

- Recourse Debt

- Asset Securitization

2

2

Many banks and other large financial institutions have purchased or started their own leasing companies

These subsidiaries are often funded entirely by the parent financial institution

The parent financial institution will typically charge the leasing subsidiary an internal interest rate

3

Brokering

Broker acts as intermediary between the lessee and the funding source

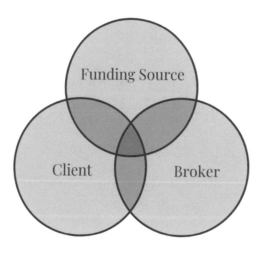

4

4

Brokering

Advantages	Disadvantages
• Little to no economic risk except for reps and warranties in the broker agreement • No servicing platform required	• Broker's profit is limited to the upfront commission paid on the transaction • Servicing relationship is transferred to funding source

5

5

Discounting

- Lessor sells remaining rents of a lease to a funding source

- Lessor retains ownership of the equipment

- Value of the rents is determined by discounting the future rents to their present value

- May be with or without recourse

  If with recourse, the purchaser of the rental stream has full or partial recourse against the lessor in case of lessee default

6

6

Discounting

Advantages	Disadvantages
Lower cost of funds	Significant reps and warranty clauses
Greater flexibility and more control	Lessor may retain some or all of the risk
Brand identity	May require working capital
Increased revenue (residual, interim rent, etc.)	Upfront profit could be less than a brokered deal
Lessor retains customer relationship	

7

Discounting

When discounting a stream on a non-recourse basis, the lessor typically represents and warrants:

1. Lease is valid and enforceable

2. Equipment has been delivered

3. Lessor has title to the equipment

4. UCC filing has been made in a timely matter

8

Recourse Debt

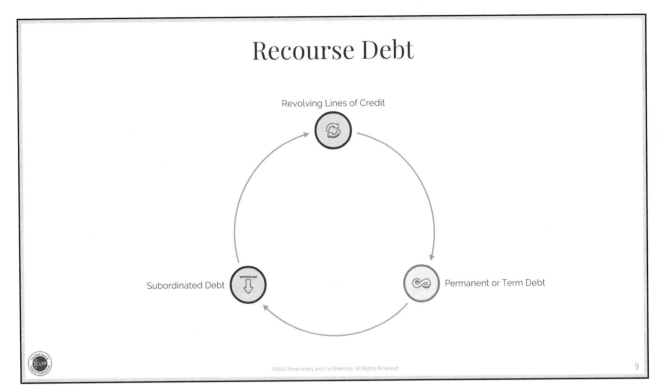

9

Recourse Debt

Revolving Lines of Credit

- Two types – Traditional Credit Facility, Warehouse Line

- Lender does not usually underwrite, fund, or take a security interest in individual transactions

- Lender requires the lessor to stay consistent with their underwriting/credit policy

- Typically supplied by a bank and the rate is tied to an index (e.g., Prime or LIBOR)

- Lender files a blanket lien against all of lessor's assets

10

10

Recourse Debt

Revolving Lines of Credit

Traditional Credit Facility

Used to fund leases to be held in the lessor's portfolio on the lessor's balance sheet

Terms are typically 1-2 years and typically renew

Terms are not tied to the duration of the underlying leases in the portfolio

Warehouse Line

Used to temporarily fund leases or "warehouse" them until a final funding source is used

Deals may be held on the line from 3-9 months

11

Recourse Debt

Term Debt

Provided by a bank and used for long-term basis

The duration of the loan is often tied to the maturity of the underlying leases

The interest rate is typically fixed at commencement

Lender files a lien against the pool of assets securing the loan

Subordinated Debt

Is junior and ranks behind (gets paid back after others are whole) any senior Traditional Credit Facility, Warehouse Line or Term Debt in case of bankruptcy or liquidation

Higher interest rate to compensate for risk

12

Recourse Debt

Advantages

Allows lessor to retain the long-term economic benefits of holding leases (early termination, residuals, renewal income, fees, interim rent)

Control and flexibility over credit, underwriting, and funding of transactions

Disadvantages

Greater risk

Limited capital

Increase in back-office expenses (labor, systems, etc.)

13

How to Qualify for Debt

- ## Track Record

  Lenders typically want to see a minimum of 1 year or more of validation of success with the credit model and performance

- ## Financial Strength/Equity

  Lenders look to equity to mitigate risk associated with unforeseen losses between the value of the assets and the amount borrowed

  High leverage ratios are perceived as higher risk which influences the pricing and availability of debt

  May be in the form of paid in capital or retained earnings

14

Asset Securitization

- Used to describe the aggregation of similar types of assets (equipment leases) into a legal structure

- Assets are used as collateral to support a bond or note

15

15

Asset Securitization

Advantages

Low cost of funds

Scale and depth of funding – ability to borrow amounts larger than lines of credit allow

Potential off-balance sheet treatment of debt

Access to the capital markets

Disadvantages

Expertise (especially legal)

High expenses associated with process

Very time-consuming to set up

Uniformity within the portfolio

Complex accounting system required

16

16

Lease Syndication

- A form of indirect origination, it is the sale and/or assignment of all or part of a lease or loan transaction and may include newly originated deals or groups of transactions from seasoned portfolios

- Equipment finance companies set up separate functions to deal with the buying (Buy Desk) and selling (Sell Desk) of transactions

17

Benefits of Lease Syndication

- Allows the equipment finance company to manage risk by credit or segment and to continue to service customer relationships and provide solutions for customers while managing exposure and concentration

- It may be less expensive to originate indirectly as it requires less staff to build this origination channel

- Syndication may also be a means to gain market intelligence to understand the terms and conditions that are accepted in the market

18

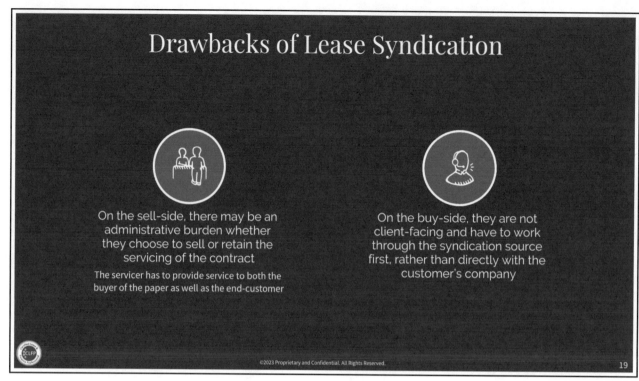

Drawbacks of Lease Syndication

On the sell-side, there may be an administrative burden whether they choose to sell or retain the servicing of the contract

The servicer has to provide service to both the buyer of the paper as well as the end-customer

On the buy-side, they are not client-facing and have to work through the syndication source first, rather than directly with the customer's company

19

19

Portfolio Acquisition

- The process of acquiring portfolios from other finance companies

- May be on a one-off basis or an ongoing basis

20

20

Regulatory Compliance

21

State Regulations

- **Electronic Recycling**
  Fees on purchasing of electronic devices

- **Security Breach**
  Notification if there is a breach of personal information

- **Automatic Renewal (Evergreen)**
  Some states regulate the renewal or end of contract terms

- **CA Finance Lenders Law**
  More details on next slide

- **Usury**
  Regulates the maximum interest rate

- **Licensing / Being in "Good Standing"**
  Covered in Credit section

22

22

California Finance Lenders Law (CFLL)

- Written in 1994
- Requires finance lenders to be licensed for transacting business
- Defines a "Finance Lender" as any person who is engaged in the business of making consumer or commercial loans

23

Federal Regulations

- CFPB (Consumer Financial Protection Bureau)

- ECOA (Reg B)
  Unlawful to make a credit decision based on a variety of factors; also mandates a "Reg B" letter be send

- Patriot Act
  Created to help detect and prevent terrorist financing and money laundering

- OFAC
  Used by financial institutions to identify known criminals

- Service Organization Controls Framework
  Used to ensure that 3rd party service companies hired by banks have adequate controls in place regarding security, etc.

- FinCEN
  Institutions must search their database for connections to known criminals

25

Funding

- Final phase of the origination process

- Executed documents are audited to authenticate customer, ensure completeness, verify accuracy, and to look for signs of fraud

- Funds are released to equipment supplier

26

26

Standard Funding Package

Includes:

- Invoice

- Verification of Executed Documents
  Wet signature
  eSignature

- Insurance

- Delivery and Acceptance (D&A)

- UCC

- Verbal Verification

- Tax Treatment

- Equipment Inspection

- Driver's License

27

27

Titled Funding Package

May also include:

- Invoice/Notarize Bill of Sale

- Power of Attorney (POA)

- Title/Manufactur Statement of Origin (MSO)

- Notary

- Driver's License (Confirm Commercial Driver's License)

28

28

Verification of Executed Documents

- Regardless of signing method, document packages are checked to verify the following:
  - Executed documents are the originals
  - Each document is signed by the proper authority
  - Document language is not crossed out, erased or modified
  - Resolution documents (if required) are properly signed for the customer entity type and transaction size

29

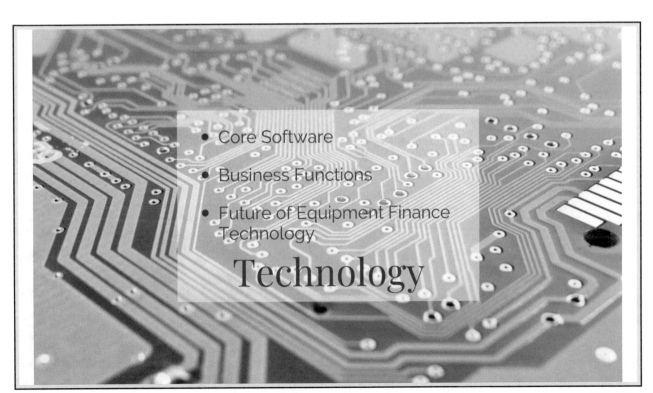

- Core Software
- Business Functions
- Future of Equipment Finance Technology

Technology

Future of Equipment Finance Technology

 Be aware
As technology changes, keep apprised of emerging trends and options

 Differentiate
Technology is a critical means to set your company apart and find solutions for customers

 Choose
Work with vendors and partners who strive to keep current

 Future-Proofing
Ensure that new solutions grow with your company

 Evolve
Building a strong digital foundations keeps relevancy and allows for better customer experience

31

Software

Core System of Record

- **CRM**
  System of record for tracking activity with contacts

- **Origination**
  System of record for quoting, credit application through documentation and funding

- **Portfolio Management (Accounting and Servicing)**
  System of record for funded and booked leases

32

Business Functions

3rd Party Services

UCC, tax calculation, credit bureaus, etc.

Data Repository, Reporting, Analytic Tools

The ability to pull information from multiple systems to analyze data to help businesses operate and grow

Content Management

Online content storage system for accessing documents, details to consider:

Security

Redundancy

Audit tracking

Findability

Corporate Support Systems

Customer Service

While customer service may often be thought as the back office or booked transaction consideration, customer experience is key throughout the ENTIRE lifecycle of the customer experience.

Pre-Booking Customer Service

Sales & Credit

Matching the borrower with the right equipment and financing solution

Documentation

Explaining and negotiating the documents

Funding

Tying up loose ends to get the transaction closed

35

35

Post-Booking Customer Service

- Payoff Requests
- Early Termination Payoffs
- End of Term
- Renewals
- Legal/Liquidation
- Sales and Property Taxes
- Account Inquiries

- Contract Adjustments
- Contract Assumptions
- Proactive Payment Relief Scenarios
- Billing and Collections
- Insurance
- Title Management
- Account Reconciliations

36

36

Insurance Administration

Insurance is used to pay for those losses that are both accidental and unexpected

Property Insurance

Lessor to be named as loss payee

Should be sufficient to compensate lessor for loss of its equipment

Liability Insurance

Lessor to be named as additional insured as to protect itself from a claim being made against them as a result of physical injury from the equipment

Insurance Binders

Temporary document used as proof of insurance and confirmation that the customer has applied to purchase an insurance policy

Insurance Certificate

Issued by the insurance agent of the company confirming that the borrower has the necessary coverage

Force-Placed/Automatic Insurance

If the borrower fails to provide required insurance coverage, the lessor reserves the right to buy adequate coverage and charge the borrower

37

Title Management

Perfection of titles is another aspect of contract servicing

Requirements

Requirements vary state to state, and depend on the age of the equipment. Understanding nuances is key.

Internal policies

Will you finance tax and registration fees into the transaction?

Documentation

Will the titling package be sent to the customer, or directly to the DMV?

38

The Academy for Lease & Finance Professionals

Setting the Standards of Professionalism For Over 30 years

Collections, Asset, and Portfolio Management
100 Points
29 Questions

1

Primary Responsibilities of a Collections Department

① Collection of lease contracts, residuals, taxes, insurance premiums, late charges, all other amounts due

② Recognizing the signals of possible delinquencies

③ Knowing which collection practices are lawful and efficient

④ Keeping losses to a minimum

⑤ Maintaining customer goodwill while protecting the company

e.g., Lessee wants to return the equipment prior to termination of lease. Collector reminds that the lease is non-cancelable.

e.g., Lessee refuses to make payment due to faulty equipment. Collector reminds that the lessor makes no warranty and any issues should be brought to the vendor's attention.

2

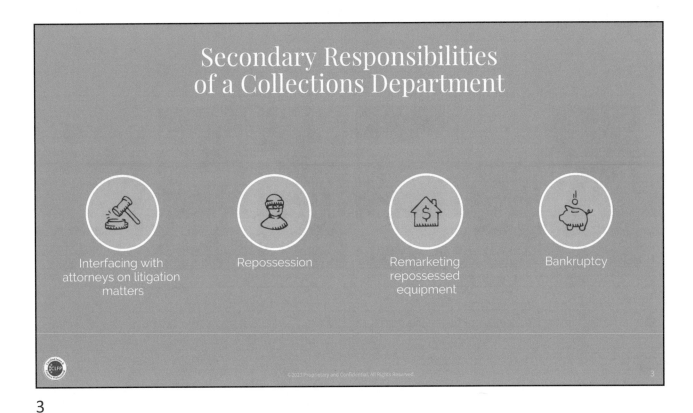

3

4

Bankruptcy Chapters

Chapter 7	Chapter 9	Chapter 11	Chapter 12	Chapter 13	Chapter 15
Personal or business liquidation of assets	Cities, Towns, Villages, etc. reorganization of debts	Business reorganization of debts	Agriculture/Farmer reorganization of debts	Individual reorganization of debts	Parties from more than one country

5

Bankruptcy Terminology

Proof of Claim
Creditors must file this affidavit stating the amount and nature of the debt in order to participate in the distribution of assets

Automatic Stay
In all cases, when a bankruptcy is filed, this is in effect as of the date of filing

Prevents collections activity

Relief of Stay
Lessor asks court for relief of the automatic stay to pick up the equipment

Filed by attorney

Bar Date
The last date on which a creditor may take action (file proof of claim, etc.)

Cram Down
Creditor is forced to take the value of the equipment, not the amount they were promised to be paid

Summons and Complaint
Once litigation has been initiated against a lessee, the lessee is served this by an independent process server

6

Preferences in Bankruptcy

- Payments within 90 days prior to the filing of the bankruptcy petition may be required to be returned to the bankruptcy estate if it is deemed preferential over any other creditor

- Exception is timely payments made in the ordinary course of business

7

Key Regulatory Considerations for Collectors

① **Fair Debt Collection Practices Act (FDCPA)**

The main federal law that governs debt collection practices. The FDCPA prohibits debt collection companies from using abusive, unfair or deceptive practices to collect debts.

② **National Automated Clearing House Association (NACHA)**

An organization that establishes the standards and rules followed by financial institutions for transferring payments.

8

Key Metrics Used in a Collections Department

- **Static Pool**

  Measures the characteristics of a specific transaction or pool of transactions originated during a set time frame

- **Roll Rate**

  Percentage of lessees who become increasingly delinquent on their accounts

- **Annualized Charge-Off Rates**

  The amount representing the difference between gross charge-offs and any subsequent recoveries of delinquent debt. Often a percentage representing that amount of debt that a company believes it will never collect compared to average receivables.

9

Signs of Delinquency

- Broken promises

- Equipment returned

- Ignored communications

- Payment not received

- Sudden change in pay habits

- Changes in company management

- Adverse economic trends in lessee's industry

- Labor disputes

- Property taxes not paid promptly

- Insurance cancellation

10

Reasons for Delinquency

- Overlooked due date
- Lease terms misunderstood
- Equipment problems
- Payment priorities
- Seasonal slow downs
- Catastrophic occurrence

- Internal accounting issues
- Personal financial difficulties
- Failing business
- Fraud
- Bankruptcy

11

11

Who to Discuss the Delinquency With

- Personal guarantors
- Point of contact on lease application

- Accounts payable
- CFO/COO/Controlle
- Other officers

12

12

Repossession

May be Voluntary, Involuntary, or by Writ of Possession	"Self-Help," the repossessing of equipment by the lessor is legal, but lessor may be liable if: It occurs over lessee's protest Causes a disturbance of the peace Causes physical injury or property damage Occurs in absence of expressed consent Occurs unsupervised on lessee's property

13

Alternatives to Repossession

① **Offer partial payments**
A tool that should be carefully managed to achieve the goal of bringing an account current.

② **Extension agreement – rewrite lease to make up for missed payments later**

③ **Change due dates - take monthly cash flow into account**

④ **Recovery agreements**
An agreement between lessor and vendor to remarket equipment

⑤ **Forbearance agreements**
The lessor gives the lessee breathing room in exchange for more favorable terms

⑥ **Transfer and assumption**
A third-party steps in to make the payments while the original lessee is secondarily liable

⑦ **Obtain judgment and enforce against Personal Guarantor – Federally Guaranteed Assets exempt (IRA, Retirement Accounts, 401k)**

14

Commercially Reasonable Sale

Required under Article 9

- Lessor must provide written notice to lessee, guarantors and junior secured creditors

- May be by public auction

- Notice of sale must be published in a paper in the county where sale is held at least 5 days prior to sale

- If not deemed "Commercially Reasonable" the lessor forfeits their rights to pursue the lessee for any deficiency balance

15

15

Portfolio Management

THE CONTINUOUS EVALUATION OF THE NATURE & PERFORMANCE
OF A LEASE PORTFOLIO, ALLOWING MANAGEMENT TO
DETERMINE FUTURE MARKETING, UNDERWRITING AND
FUNDING STRATEGY

16

Cross-Functional Requirements

Origination

Proper due diligence and data validation to ensure accurate sourcing

Credit

Complete and accurate information for proper risk analysis

Documentation

Complete and accurate document inputs to maximize collection ability

17

17

Portfolio Segmentation is Key

(1) Origination Source

(4) Lease Type

(2) Credit Evaluation Method

(5) Lease Term

(3) Special Credit Program

(6) Industry

18

18

Performance Indicators to Observe

Credit Risk Indicators

Delinquency %

$$\frac{30 - 60 - 90 \; Day \; Delinquencies}{Total \; Receivables}$$

FREQUENCY OF DELINQUENCIES OR DEFAULTS
30, 60, 90-DAY RECEIVABLES AGING
AMOUNT OF CHARGE-OFFS OR DEFAULTS
TIMING OF DEFAULTS
COLLECTION/RECOVERY COSTS
AMOUNT OF RECOVERY NET OF COSTS

Residual Performance %

$$\frac{Total \; Residual \; Value \; Collected}{Estimated \; Booked \; Residual}$$

19

Performance Indicators to Observe

Financial Risk Indicators

Net Interest Yield

$$Gross \; Yield \; - \; IDC \; or \; Origination \; Cost$$

Interest Margin

$$Gross \; Yield \; - \; Cost \; of \; Debt$$

GROSS INTEREST YIELD
NET INTEREST YIELD
INTEREST MARGIN
INTEREST RATE RISK
WEIGHTED AVERAGE YIELDS
TERM LENGTH AND RUNOFF RATE
RESIDUAL VALUE PERFORMANCE
EARLY PAYOFFS
SERVICING COSTS
AMOUNT AND TYPE OF FEE INCOME

20

Performance Patterns to Observe

- Business Risk Indicators
  - Market competition
  - Concentration risk
  - Economic trends
  - Availability of cost of capital and debt
  - Availability and expertise of personnel
  - State-specific legal remedies
  - Documentation thoroughness
  - Application of performance indicators

- Concentration Risk Examples
  - Industry
  - Equipment type
  - Origination source
  - Geography

21

21

Ways for Portfolio Managers to Mitigate Risk

- Knowledge of the following areas can help ensure compliance and minimize risk
  Uniform Commercial Code (UCC)
  Vehicle Titling Laws
  FASB Regulations
  Local Usury Laws
  Sales, Use and Personal Property Tax

22

22

Asset Management Responsibilities

- Equipment valuation

- Equipment appraisal

- Residual valuation

- Equipment recovery

- Inventory management

- Secondary remarketing

23

Equipment Valuation Types

- Fair Market Value (FMV)

  The amount for which the asset could be bought or sold, in a transaction between a willing buyer and a willing seller in an open market

- Orderly Liquidation Value (OLV)

  An estimate of the gross amount that the tangible assets would fetch in an auction-style liquidation

- Absolute Value

  A valuation method that looks only at the asset's intrinsic value and does not compare to other assets

- Forced Liquidation Value (FLV)

  The amount of money that a company will receive if it sold its assets in an auction immediately

- Relative Value (RV)

  A method of determining an asset's value that takes into account the value of similar assets

- Repossession Value

  A valuation method to determine if there is enough value in the equipment to warrant repossession

- Residual Value

  The value of the equipment at the end of the lease term

24

Asset Manager Involvement by Lease Stage

① Pre-Funding
- Assign FMV, OLV and FLV of the equipment
- Determine the estimated residual value
- Ensure the lease term aligns with the asset value and useful life

② Post-Funding
- Profitability monitoring
- Residual value review
- Asset remarketing at the end of the lease
- Asset disposal at the end of the lease

③ Default Scenarios
- Asset repossession
- Determine liquidation value
- Determine cost of asset recovery
- Determine whether asset recovery makes sense

25

Equipment Valuation Criteria

Equipment Type & Age

Servicing Requirements

Depreciable Life

Manufacturer, Make & Model

Intended Utilization

26

Possible Residual Review Outcomes

- **Write-down**
  A reduction in the value of an asset

- **Write-off**
  The complete elimination of an asset

27

27

Default Considerations

Increase in Bad Debt Reserves
Deficiencies in equipment values, especially those related to defaults, may cause the bank or lessor to have to reserve larger amounts for future charge-offs

Tripping of Financial Covenants
Write-offs affect cash flow, and can cause the lender to fall outside of financial covenants

Loss of Funding Sources
Funding sources will be reluctant to lend to those who do not properly manage asset risk

28

28

Legal Impact

Important Questions to Ask

- Does the customer require the equipment to stay in business?

- Should the lessor involve the guarantor(s)?

- Should the lessor recover the equipment or sue the customer?

- If a lawsuit is necessary, should a replevin be considered?

  Replevin is a lawsuit seeking an order from a judge requiring the lessee to surrender the equipment at a certain date, time and place

29

29